MADAGASCAR

Jay Heale

MARSHALL CAVENDISH
New York • London • Sydney

Reference edition published 1998 by
Marshall Cavendish Corporation
99 White Plains Road
Tarrytown
New York 10591

© Times Editions Pte Ltd 1998

Originated and designed by
Times Books International, an imprint of
Times Editions Pte Ltd

Printed in Singapore

Library of Congress Cataloging-in-Publication Data:
Heale, Jay.
    Madagascar / Jay Heale.
      p. cm.—(Cultures of the World)
    Includes bibliographical references (p.) and index.
    Summary: Introduces the geography, history, religious
beliefs, government, and people of Madagascar.
    ISBN 0-7614-0693-X
    1. Madagascar—Juvenile literature. [1. Madagascar.]
I. Title. II. Series.
D469.M28H43 1998
969.1—dc21   97–16569
                CIP
                AC

INTRODUCTION

MADAGASCAR HAS BEEN CALLED "the island at the end of the earth" by a Malagasy poet because, beyond its southern tip, there is only ocean all the way to the Antarctic. When someone born in Madagascar goes abroad, he takes with him a small packet of red earth. This is to ensure his eventual return to the Great Red Island, with its soil and rivers the color of blood. More often, they do not leave at all. One citizen remarked, "The temptation to remain withdrawn from the world is an island characteristic, and it is still very strong here."

Although the facts in this book are presented in separate chapters, so much in Madagascar is interwoven. History is a part of the people, the economy affects the lifestyle and lack of leisure, and the restrictions of what is *fady* ("FAH-di," or forbidden) extend far beyond religious beliefs into every aspect of living and dying. Renowned for its unique plants and wildlife, Madagascar should be better known for the gentle courtesy of its friendly people.

CONTENTS

Life is simple in the villages, and it is common to see people carrying goods slung at one or both ends of a pole supported on their shoulder.

CONTENTS

These prickly *didierea* are unique to Madagascar. Despite their spiny appearance, they are not cacti but trees.

GEOGRAPHY

MOST PEOPLE KNOW OF MADAGASCAR only as a large island off the coast of Africa. In the process of continental drift, it broke away from the mainland about 165 million years ago and has been cut off since, which explains why 85% of its plants and animals are exclusive to the island. The mainland of Africa now lies about 250 miles (400 km) to the west, across the Mozambique Channel.

Madagascar is the fourth largest island in the world (after Greenland, New Guinea, and Borneo), with a landmass of 226,598 square miles (586,889 square km), including its offshore islands. One thousand miles (1,609 km) long, Madagascar is approximately twice the size of the state of Arizona, but only has one-fifth of its population. There are no particularly high mountains, but a high plateau ranging in height from 2,400 to 4,430 feet (731–1,350 m) runs down the north-south axis like a backbone.

Four-fifths of the population of about 13.5 million live on what they can produce from the land. When there is not enough land for growing rice or grazing cattle, trees in the remaining forest are cut down and the timber used as fuel. The bared earth is then subjected to erosion, and the topsoil that could have supported better crops is washed away into the ocean. It is an ecological disaster, especially when one considers that the dwindling forests are the homes of creatures not found elsewhere in the world.

Politically the island is divided into Antananarivo (the capital and itself a province) in the central highlands and six other provinces: Mahajanga

Above: **Madagascar is home to about a quarter of the world's plant and animal kingdom.**

Opposite: **Western Madagascar receives rainfall for only four months of the year.**

Rice, a staple food, being planted in the highlands.

to the northwest, Toamasina ("toor-MAS-in") to the northeast, Antsiranana on the northern tip, Toliara on the southwest, Fianarantsoa on the southeast, and Tôlañaro on the southern tip.

CENTRAL HIGHLANDS

A high plateau forms the spine of Madagascar. This is the land of the Merina, the most numerous and once most powerful of the Malagasy tribes. It is still the most prosperous and cultured area in the country. Rolling hills form pastures for zebu cattle, while the valleys are terraced with rice fields. In the west, the hills turn bare and dry; in the east, forested escarpments lead to the narrow coastal plain. At Périnet Reserve, reached by road from Antananarivo, there is a population of indri, the largest of the lemur species. Semiprecious stones such as jasper, rose quartz, agate, and amethyst are found in small quantities in the mountains. Snow is not uncommon on the highlands in the winter.

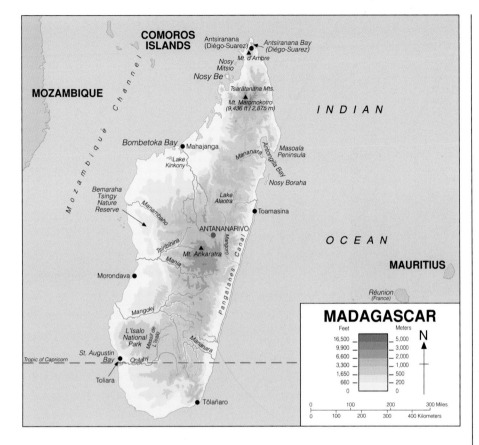

ANTANANARIVO

The capital of Madagascar, Antananarivo (usually shortened to Tana), is a growing city of more than a million people. It has the country's only international airport. The city sprawls over a curving ridge with the *Zoma* ("ZOO-mah," or market area) on one side, and Lake Anosy and a World War I memorial on the other.

The road system is so complex that, as one resident puts it, "a compass would get confused, let alone a visitor." The long, straight Avenue de l'Indépendence runs through the poorer, lower area; changes its name to Avenue du 26 Juin as it passes the market area; then travels through a tunnel under the Upper Town to merge with L. Jean Ralaimongo Road beside the lake. There, drivers can turn left to the soccer stadium or right to the Hilton Hotel, the only skyscraper in town.

Antananarivo's development began under French colonial administration in the late 19th and early 20th century.

In the Upper Town lies the presidential palace, with government buildings clustered around it. Some of the better hotels, like the Colbert and Radama, are in this area as is the newly established tourist office that distributes free maps and advice.

Higher, on the skyline, are the four towers of the Queen's Palace (known as the Rova) that was gutted by fire in November 1995. All that remains are rows of arched windows gaping at the sky. Fortunately, many of the historic items on display were saved from the fire and restoration on the palace has begun. On this higher ridge are several Catholic churches, four of them dedicated to Malagasy martyrs, and many schools.

THE SOUTH

The southern areas are a mixture of semidesert, coral-fringed beaches, nature reserves, scrub-covered hills, and the stark sandstone peaks of L'Isalo National Park. This is the driest part of Madagascar—a "spiny" desert where baobabs, aloes, and spiky green octopus trees (similar to but unrelated to cactus) live in a tangle of thorny scrub. Tough, dark-skinned people tend cattle in a hard, dry land. Large areas have been cleared to grow sisal, which stands in spiky green rows in the red soil.

The French introduced the prickly pear cactus from Mexico, and it is grown as natural fencing and used for feeding cattle. Fragments of fossilized eggs belonging to the extinct "elephant bird" are sometimes found in this region. Two popular nature reserves are the Berenty and Kaleta parks, which provide a refuge for ringtail and brown lemurs as well as the creamy-white sifaka lemurs and huge fruit bats.

Only 5 miles (8 km) east of this semidesert, separated by a mountain range, is a tropical east coast jungle and the breezy town of Tôlañaro. It is also known as Fort Dauphin, taking its name from the French-built fort there that now lies in ruins. Residents of the town prefer the Malagasy name, but most guidebooks retain the French colonial name. The town is built on a peninsula with a small harbor on one side, overlooked by the red-painted Palais de Justice. This stone church is used during the week as a classroom to house an overflow of students from the nearby school. A large crucifix stands on a hill above the town. Toward the sea, a newly built mosque stands beside the crumbling ruins of the fort. Hotels and restaurants in the area cater to tourists.

In the lush, green undergrowth (climatically part of the eastern coastal strip) can be found the rare, three-cornered palm and the carnivorous pitcher plant that lives on insects.

Tôlañaro in southeastern Madagascar, facing the Indian Ocean, is also called Fort Dauphin, after the French East India Company fort of the same name.

Brightly colored flowers of the pitcher plant, which grows wild in eastern Madagascar, attract and trap insects in search of nectar. The plant's enzymes break the proteins of trapped insects down into a form it can absorb.

THE EAST

The eastern part of Madagascar, with its almost straight coastline, is known as the Whale Highway because of the migrating humpback whales that stop there to breed. It is also nicknamed the Pirate Coast because of legends about the presence of pirates in the area. An inland waterway, called the Pangalanes Canal, runs parallel to the shore. This is a 375-mile (603-km) chain of lakes and canals that was once a busy route for canoes carrying great loads of fruit and vegetables. It is now clogged with reeds and water hyacinths and used mainly for local fishing.

The eastern shoreline is a fertile area drenched with tropical rains from December to March. It is also fast becoming known as the Cyclone Coast. One year the island was hit by 13 cyclones. Historically, the most destructive cyclones include one that severely damaged the city of Toamasina in 1927, a storm in 1986 that tore across the island of Nosy Boraha ("noosh bor-AH"), also called Sainte Marie, and Cyclone Geralda, which struck the same area in February 1994, wrecking roads and railways and leaving 500,000 people homeless. The cyclones, combined with centuries of slash-and-burn destruction of the rainforests, have eroded the steep slopes, causing gaping red holes known as *lavaka* ("LA-vak").

Toamasina on the east coast is Madagascar's largest port, exporting sugar and coffee. It is connected to the capital by road, rail, and air. The town has a population of over 100,000 and is a popular holiday resort for the Malagasy. Nosy Boraha, farther north, boasts the world's only "pirate graveyard." As it is unlikely that any of the famous pirates of Madagascar are buried here, it does not matter much that wind and rain have made most of the carved inscriptions illegible. The country's largest lake, Alaotra, was once in a wooded area with rice paddies around the lake. Then, as has happened throughout much of Madagascar, the trees were cut down to provide land to grow crops and graze cattle. The soil eroded and washed into the lake, which is now less than a third of its original size. The town of Ambatondrazaka was once next to the lake but is now 15 miles (24 km) from the water.

High rainfall makes this the greenest part of the island. Cloves, vanilla, coffee, and fruit are grown for export, and rare orchids flourish. The shoreline is picturesque, although swimmers have to be wary of sharks. Sometimes gold cups and coins are found washed up on the beach, and tales of buried pirate treasure persist.

The jungle is under threat from land cultivation and the effects of modernization.

The island of Nosy Be was one of two early French footholds near the mainland. The other was the island of Nosy Boraha, also known as Sainte Marie.

THE NORTH

Much of northern Madagascar is cut off by the rugged Tsarätanana mountains that contain the island's highest peak, Maromokotro (9,436 ft/ 2,875 m). These mountains cause varied weather conditions. The area around Antsiranana (also known as Diégo-Suarez) on the east is dry, while the island-strewn coastline around Nosy Be in the west has a higher rainfall.

Antsiranana has one of the finest deepwater harbors in the world. During its history, the port has accommodated slavers, pirates, a French naval base built in 1885, and British occupation during World War II. A legend tells of the existence of a 17th century republic called Libertalia, founded here by pirates.

Local industries include shipbuilding, tuna fishing, and salt extraction. Inland, there is the Amber Mountain National Park, a volcanic massif covered with forest. Picturesque waterfalls with malachite kingfishers and bats attract tourists, while the dense trees conceal chameleons, orchids, and endangered species of lemur. Crocodiles live in the humid underground caves, and there are nine species of shrimp and seven varieties of bats, according to studies initiated by the World Wildlife Fund (WWF).

Farther south is Ankarana, an area of weirdly shaped, razor-sharp limestone pinnacles known as *tsingy* ("TSING-i," meaning "spikes"). These are considered sacred by the local people, who have buried several of their kings in one of the caves there.

14

Nosy Be, meaning "big island," is a popular tourist destination. The increasing numbers of tourists from abroad pronounce this "NOSS-i BAY," but the local inhabitants prefer "noosh bay." Its setting of fertile greenery, vanilla plantations, and sweet-smelling yellow ilang-ilang blossoms (used to make perfume), combined with fine beaches and stunning marine life for those keen on snorkeling, make for a perfect holiday. There are expensive hotels catering to wealthy visitors. The moneymaking atmosphere here, however, is not representative of Madagascar as a whole.

The main town on Nosy Be is Hell-Ville, named after Admiral de Hell (a former governor

Ilang-ilang blossoms, valued as a perfume base, growing on Nosy Be.

of the neighboring island of Réunion), but most visitors stay in beach hotel complexes. Excursions take tourists to Lokobe, a fragment of preserved forest, or to the highest point on the island, Mont Passot, which has deep-blue crater lakes. The smaller islands can be reached by boat. An amazing variety of coral, starfish, anemones, turtles, and fish can be found in the clear waters, and diving tours are available. The nearby island of Nosy Komba is an unofficial sanctuary for black lemurs.

THE WEST

The western slopes of Madagascar were once thickly forested; today only clumps of deciduous trees on dry, open savanna grassland remain. From the air the land looks crinkled, with long looping rivers that divide and join again. The Sakalava people live here; their kingdom, which once

Fishing along the west coast to supplement the traditional diet staples of rice and cassava.

dominated the entire region, was the most powerful in Malagasy history. The two main towns are Mahajanga and Morondava, although the areas are now sparsely populated and, in some rocky districts, uninhabited. The coast has mangrove swamps, sweeping sandy beaches, and coral reefs. The endangered Madagascar fish eagle, one of the world's rarest raptors, can sometimes be seen.

Mahajanga, at the mouth of the Betsiboka River, is the second largest port on the island, well sited for trade with Africa and the Middle East. Founded probably by Arabs, Mahajanga was once a major supply depot for slaves. It is a hot, busy, windblown town with a mixed population and strong business community, many of them Indian. Many churches and mosques can be found.

Local industries include meat and vegetable-oil processing, and the growth and export of coffee. At the end of the summer, people like to burn the coarse, old grass to generate fresh new growth for the cattle in the spring. Unfortunately, when the grass is burned, there is nothing to stop the soil from washing away in heavy rain. The sea off Mahajanga is stained blood-red by silt from the Betsiboka River. Some Mahajangans own holiday chalets on the beach at Amborovy, near an area of strangely eroded red and mauve rock shapes, known as Cirque Rouge.

Much farther south lies Morondava. Once grand with seaside villas, it suffers from encroaching sand and increasing poverty. The sea gains at least 3 feet (about one meter) every year in spite of concrete breakwaters and rocks held together with wire nets to protect the shoreline. Fishers venture out in dugout canoes trailing nets, coconut palms bend against the wind, and inland, children in tattered clothes tend herds of zebu cattle among baobab trees with huge trunks. There is a soccer stadium, two discotheques, and several restaurants serving fresh seafood. Although rain falls here only four months of the year, there are areas of intense cultivation where huge, cleared circles are supplied with rotating water systems.

Bemahara Tsingy, Madagascar's largest nature reserve at 375,592 acres (152,115 hectares), lies between Mahajanga and Morondava and has an almost inaccessible maze of limestone needles and canyons as well as remote tombs of the Vazimba people, reputedly the country's earliest inhabitants. Toliara, in the southwest, is a fishing port and sisal-processing center. Crops such as peanuts, rice, and cotton are grown.

A major product of the southern region is sisal, used to make sacking, rope, and matting.

CLIMATE

The climate is mostly tropical. The prevailing trade winds bring rain from the east, while monsoon winds blow from the northwest, resulting in more rain in the north than in the south. Rainfall varies from torrential storms on the east coast during February and March to dry conditions on the southwest, which may receive only 2 inches (5 cm) of rain a year. In general, the summer months from November to April are the wettest, with northwest air currents bringing the rain. Average summer temperatures range from 77°F (25°C) around the capital to 86°F (30°C) on the coast.

BAOBAB TREES

The baobab is sometimes described as an "upside-down tree" because it looks as if someone has plucked it from the earth and shoved it back in with its roots in the air. In fact, it may be wrong to classify it as a tree at all because it is a succulent that stores water in its trunk. Unlike most trees, it does not die when the bark is stripped off. The bark is used to make fibrous cloth, baskets, strings for musical instruments, and waterproof hats. The lightweight wood is used for fishing floats and canoes. The leaves are eaten like spinach, the seeds provide oil, the empty seed husks are used as utensils, and the pulp makes a refreshing drink.

There are eight species of baobab in the world: six are found only in Madagascar, and the others in Africa and Australia. They can live for several thousand years, so many of the baobabs on Madagascar were alive long before man arrived on the island. An impressive avenue of giant baobabs stands near Morondava, and tourists are taken to view two baobabs entwined like lovers.

Temperatures in the central highlands can drop to freezing during winter nights from June to August.

FLORA AND FAUNA

Madagascar's unique plants and animals are a major tourist attraction. Approximately 10,000 plants have been identified, representing a quarter of the plants found in the entire African region. Madagascar not only has a record number of species unique to the island, but because of the continuing loss of forest cover, it also has more endangered species than any other country in the world. For the Malagasy rice cultivation and

The rosy periwinkle is the basis of a drug that can cure childhood leukemia.

cattle rearing are two of their most vital economic activities, and these cannot be carried out in a forest. As a result, the forests have been cut down steadily for hundreds of years. About 15% of the original forests remain and another 800 square miles (2,070 square km) are slashed and burned each year.

There are now 37 protected areas (nature reserves and national parks) maintained in partnership with the World Wildlife Fund and traditional healers work with a team of Malagasy students to catalog the wealth of medicinal plants in the northern forests. The rosy periwinkle, for example, provides an essential compound used to treat childhood leukemia. Overseas agencies, such as the US Agency for International Development and UNESCO, also help with funding ecological preservation.

Among Madagascar's most famous mammals are the lemurs, which have apparently undergone little evolutionary change since the Eocene period about 50 million years ago. Another unusual animal is the tenrec, which looks like a tiny hedgehog with yellow and black stripes and bristling spines that rattle when it is angry. Among the 33 species of tenrec are some that are furry. The largest is the size of a rabbit and is considered a food delicacy. There are 28 species of bats, including fruit bats, or flying foxes. Among the mongoose-like carnivores is the fossa, which can be as large and as vicious as a puma. A rabbit-sized, giant jumping rat, not unlike a wallaby, can also be found.

In the reptile world, Madagascar claims to be home to two-thirds of the world's species of chameleons. A chameleon's eyes swivel independently, allowing it to look forwards and backwards at the same time. A Malagasy

Madagascar has many types of chameleons, lizards that can change the color of their skin to blend in with their natural surroundings.

TREES FOR LIFE

The *Madagascar Program* of the World Wide Fund for Nature published the following quote by Chief Bakary, from the village of Ajavimihavanana in northern Madagascar, as he shared with his people a new appreciation of tree conservation: "Last night, our ancestors spoke to me in a vision. They revealed that God gave us four important trees for life. He gave us the mango tree for its sweet fruit and plentiful shade. He gave us the kapok (silk cotton) tree because we can use the fruit fibers to weave mats to rest and meditate on. He gave us the avocado tree so that we can sell its fruit and make a profit. And finally, God gave us the jackfruit tree as a symbol of friendship. By knocking on the fruit, we can tell if it is ripe by the sound it makes. Therefore the jackfruit is our friend because it can communicate with us."

LEMURS

The ancestors of the lemurs on Madagascar may have drifted from the African mainland on logs. Without any large predators on the island, they evolved freely and today there are varieties ranging from the mouse lemurs to giant, bearlike lemurs. Some species became extinct after man arrived on the island. The remaining 30 species and 40 subspecies are constantly threatened by slash-and-burn clearing of the forests.

Lemurs are not monkeys, although they are the closest living descendants of the common ancestor of the monkeys. Other survivors of this line are the bush babies of Africa. Monkeys are more clever than lemurs, which are more primitive and gentle. Lemurs live largely on fruit and insects. Their long noses give them a highly developed sense of smell. About half the 30 species are nocturnal, including the strangest of all, the aye-aye. It looks like a large-headed squirrel with bat's ears, a fox's tail, and tiny hands with a bony middle finger that it uses to dig for grubs or pick out the kernels from nuts.

Unfortunately, many Malagasy believe that the aye-aye brings bad luck. They are afraid that the "crooked finger" may point out the next person to die, so many aye-aye have been killed. Aye-aye have also incurred the fury of farmers because they have a sweet tooth and raid coconuts and sugarcane. There is a protected aye-aye reserve on the island of Nosy Mangabe.

proverb says, "Be like the chameleon—keep one eye on the past and one eye on the future." There are also fringed geckos, boa constrictors, several species of tortoise and marine turtles, and over 300 butterflies and moths. Birds are harder to spot. Amongst the rarer birds is the Madagascar flufftail.

Madagascar is considered one of the richest floral kingdoms in the world, with estimates of the number of species ranging from 7,000 to 12,000. There are, for example, 60 species of aloe and 1,000 of orchids, many of which grow on trees, where they live in harmony (not as parasites) with the tree, collecting water as it runs down the trunk.

HISTORY

ALTHOUGH THE EARLY history of Madagascar is is somewhat vague, it is believed that human beings first set foot on the shores of the island shortly after Jesus' birth.

Madagascar was apparently uninhabited until about 2,000 years ago when the first settlers arrived—not from Africa in the west as one might have guessed, but from the Malay Peninsula and Indonesia, 4,000 miles (6,440 km) to the east. Some think that they might have sailed straight across the Indian Ocean to Madagascar. Others believe the process took longer, with explorers making their way southwest through India, Arabia, and Africa, intermarrying and acquiring their ethnic mix along the way. Known more in local legend than in fact, these earliest inhabitants were called the Vazimba and considered the ancestral guardians of the land. Beginning in the 6th century, when Sumatra controlled trade in the Indian Ocean, more settlers, including Muslim traders, arrived. Different tribal groups began to establish control over various areas.

Above: **Fishers rigging a pirogue in Bombetoka Bay.**

Opposite: **The gateway to Ambohimanga, 12 miles (19 km) from the capital. In ancient times, a large stone was rolled across the entrance at night.**

EUROPEAN ARRIVALS

In 1500 the Portuguese were the first Europeans to arrive. They named the land the Isle of Saint Lawrence, but did not stay any longer than later arrivals, the Dutch and the English. None of them thought the island was worth colonizing. The French established a colony in 1642, but plagued with disease and attacked constantly by the local inhabitants, they left. More permanent residents were the bands of pirates operating constantly in the area, especially along the eastern shore.

In the west the Menabe tribe, with the help of firearms bought from European traders, extended their rule into the highlands as far as Bengy on the Sakalava River. Sakalava became the name of the people in that region. King Andriamisara I of the Menabe and his successor, Andriandahifotsy, came close to uniting southern and eastern Madagascar. Their successors ruled for nearly 200 years until the early 19th century.

Robert Drury, a British sailor shipwrecked on Madagascar in 1703, stayed for 16 years as a slave, royal butcher, and refugee. His journal was once regarded as a historical source, until it was determined that its editor and ghostwriter was Daniel Defoe, who had padded the sailor's story with descriptions written in 1658 by Etienne de Flacourt and added some reflections of his own. Defoe is the well-known author of the story of Robinson Crusoe.

PIRATES

When the rich hauls of the West Indies pirates began to look thin, the buccaneers of the sea diverted their attention to the trade routes around the Cape of Good Hope, to India and the East Indies. The east coast of Madagascar was an ideal base, and Nosy Boraha became their headquarters. The island is a thin strip of land with coconut-fringed beaches surrounded by shallow seas. Captain William Kidd, an English buccaneer, arrived on board his first ship, the *Adventure*, in 1695, starting a life of piracy that ended on the gallows in London. Other infamous names include another English pirate called John Avery, the American pirate Thomas Tew, and the Frenchman, Olivier Levasseur, known as La Buse (The Buzzard, or possibly The Fool). The names on the tombstones in the pirate graveyard have long since worn away, but one skull and crossbones symbol can still be seen.

On the east coast, the pirate headquarters on Nosy Boraha attracted buccaneers from far away and a 40-gun fort was built there to protect pirated goods. Ratsimilaho, the son of an English pirate and a Malagasy princess, united many of the rival coastal tribes into the empire of Betsimisaraka ("BET-si-MI-sha-rahk"), which means "those who stand together."

In 1750 his daughter Bety married a shipwrecked French corporal and Ratsimilaho gave them the island of Nosy Boraha as a wedding gift. Upon Ratsimilaho's death, Princess Bety ruled in her father's place and ceded the island to France. Her son, who ruled after her, was unable to control local uprisings and the Betsimisaraka kingdom shrank to become a single port.

Hand-colored engraving showing slave caravans on the road.

THE MERINA KINGDOMS

In the meantime the Merina ("MAIR-n") tribe was steadily increasing its domination of the central highlands, using weapons gained through trade agreements with European sea powers. In 1810 King Radama I modernized the army and with 35,000 men established the largest kingdom yet in Madagascar. Unable to defeat the Sakalava kingdom of Menabe, Radama I arranged a marriage between his daughter and the Menabe king, Ramitraho. Radama established positive relations with European powers. A Frenchman was the general of his army and an Englishman, his adviser.

During King Radama II's reign, French Roman Catholics and English Protestants vied for power, and there was a palace revolt against his European-influenced policies.

The capital was moved to Antananarivo by 1800, and the ongoing slave trade was stopped. In 1820 Britain signed a treaty recognizing Madagascar as an independent state under Merina rule. The London Missionary Society sent missionaries and converted the Merina court to Christianity. Some missionaries taught the people skills so they could become blacksmiths, carpenters, printers, or weavers.

In the 1840s Queen Ranavalona I declared Christianity illegal and killed many converts. Four churches in the capital city now stand in memory of these early martyrs. Her son, Radama II, ascended the throne in 1861 and established religious freedom. He improved the judicial system and encouraged foreign trade. Christianity became more or less official in Madagascar. However, Radama II was assassinated after only one year in office.

A FRENCH COLONY

Competing European powers played the next role in Madagascar's history. In 1890 France and Britain signed a treaty in which French control over Madagascar was recognized in return for British sovereignty in Zanzibar. The French selected Mahajanga as the base for their expeditionary force, which marched into Antananarivo. By the time they arrived in the capital on September 30, 1895, the invading force had shrunk to 4,000 men—over 11,000 had died of disease along the march. But since sickness and starvation had also struck and weakened the Merina forces, the French captured the capital. They set up a colonial administration with

Joseph Galliéni as governor-general. In 1897 the French exiled the Merina queen and turned Madagascar into a French protectorate.

Galliéni made French the official language and tried to suppress both the Malagasy language and the earlier British influence. The colonial settlers cleared the forests to make way for sugarcane, cotton, and coffee plantations. Harsh taxation resulted in forced labor for those unable to pay, and many peasants were forced to work in conditions of semi-slavery. Although the island developed under French rule and there were construction projects and economic progress, there was also an increasing resentment and desire for national independence.

During World War II, British forces occupied several major towns, including Antananarivo and the port of Diégo-Suarez, to prevent the harbor from falling into Japanese hands. Madagascar, however, was handed back to the French, led by General Charles de Gaulle. In the highland plateau, the struggle for political rights by the Merina led to an uprising in March 1947 that was crushed ruthlessly by the French army. Several thousand Malagasy were killed, and the leaders exiled. The French then began to transfer political power to the leaders of the coastal regions.

In 1958 the Malagasy people voted in a referendum to become an autonomous republic within the French community of overseas nations. Independence was granted on June 26, 1960 (now celebrated as

The French legislature passed a law making Madagascar a French colony, and General J. Galliéni arrived from France to subdue the Merina and abolish its monarchy.

Didier Ratsiraka wielded power over three terms as president (from 1975 to 1992) before being deposed. He was reelected in January 1997.

Independence Day), and Philibert Tsiranana was elected as the first president of the Malagasy Republic.

THE FIRST REPUBLIC

The recent history of Madagascar has been greatly influenced by the struggles for power between the two main ethnic groups: the *côtiers* ("COH-ti-ay," or coastal people) and the highland Merina. Although supposedly independent, Madagascar continued to be dominated by France, which stayed in control of trade and financial institutions. President Tsiranana was pro-French and refused to establish diplomatic contact with communist countries. He was disliked by the Merina because he was a côtier. The economy slumped and uprisings were suppressed as harshly as they had been under French rule.

Massive antigovernment demonstrations took place in 1972, forcing President Tsiranana to resign. The civilian government was replaced by a military one. A period of martial law followed during which a new leader, Colonel Richard Ratsimandrava, was shot dead within a week of taking office. In June 1975 the Supreme Council of the Revolution, led by Admiral Didier Ratsiraka, ushered in a Christian-Marxist one-party state, changing the name of the country from the Malagasy Republic to the Democratic Republic of Madagascar.

THE SECOND REPUBLIC

President Ratsiraka found himself president of a country with a shattered economy and a nonexistent education system. Banks, insurance companies, and major businesses were then nationalized. Ties with France were cut, and military help was welcomed from the Soviet Union. A debt crisis in 1981, however, forced Ratsiraka to rethink these reforms and return to a free-market economy. In 1982 he was reelected to a second seven-year term, but mounting unrest forced him to allow opposition parties to be introduced during the run-up to the 1989 elections. In spite of this, he was elected to a third term as president. There were widespread allegations of ballot rigging and a series of protest riots began. Amid the fall of communism in Eastern Europe and the crumbling of the Soviet Union, Ratsiraka maintained friendly relations with North Korea and made trade agreements with the apartheid government of South Africa.

The main opposition, the Forces Vives, called for general strikes. Demonstrations for democracy were staged by nearly half a million people in front of the presidential palace. The presidential guard opened fire on the demonstrators and many were killed. In November 1991 President Ratsiraka relinquished power to the prime minister, Guy Razanamary, but refused to step down from his official position.

A transitional government was formed to draft a new constitution, which was approved by a referendum in August 1992. This declared Madagascar to be a unitary state with multiparty democracy and reduced the executive powers of the president. In the subsequent presidential elections, Professor Albert Zafy (a French-trained professor of surgery and leader of the Forces Vives) was elected, ending 17 years of Ratsiraka's virtual dictatorship. Zafy became the first president of the Third Republic, and Madagascar was put on the path toward a truer democracy.

When Didier Ratsiraka came into power in 1975, he attempted to create a personality cult of his own through the publication of the Boky Mena ("BOO-ki-MAIN," or Red Book), which set out the charter of his Socialist Revolution for Madagascar, in much the same way as Colonel Muammar Qaddafi had done in Libya with his Green Book.

GOVERNMENT

FROM ITS EARLIEST HISTORY up to 1975, Madagascar has seen the rule of independent kingdoms (such as the Merina and Menabe), defeat and control by a European colonial power (France), supposed independence as a republic (while still under French domination), autocratic power-wielding by President Philibert Tsiranana, and the introduction of a Marxist one-party state by President Didier Ratsiraka. The political theory of Marxism holds that ideally a country progresses from allegiance to a local ruler (feudalism), to privately owned production (capitalism), to public ownership of a country's assets (socialism), to the eventual goal of a classless society, or communism. In Madagascar, communism brought economic ruin.

Left: **Malagasy soldiers presenting arms in a military camp in Antananarivo.**

Opposite: **Merina kings and queens lived in this palace that stands on a hill overlooking Antananarivo, a reminder of an era when the monarchy had to contend with foreign interest and domination. The palace was gutted by fire in 1995. Today all that remains is a shell.**

A small coastal community. The coastal people, or côtiers, were much less privileged than the Merina prior to French rule in Madagascar.

THE CHANGING CONSTITUTION

Annexed by France as a colony in 1896, the Malagasy Republic (as it was then called) became self-governing in 1958. The island gained full independence in 1960 and changed its name to the Democratic Republic of Madagascar in 1975. Ruled by President Didier Ratsiraka as *Le Deuxième République* (The Second Republic) from 1975 to 1992, Madagascar tried Marxism, nationalizing foreign banks and firms.

Under the 1975 constitution, there was a People's National Assembly, with 137 members elected by the people. However, a 22-member Supreme Revolutionary Council, two-thirds of whom were appointed by the president, made the most important decisions. For practical administration, the president appointed a Council of Ministers, headed by the prime minister. Those 17 years are now thought of as a dictatorship. The new constitution of August 1992 introduced a more democratic government and a number of political parties were formed.

The power to make laws rests with the National Assembly, which consists of 138 members, with 24 ministries operating under the prime minister. However, the constitution (ratified in 1993) indicates that many of these ministries are liable to be altered. There are plans to revise the number of regions in order to improve government decentralization. The intention is to divide the country into some 20 regions on a socioeconomic basis. The constitution also provides for a senate of which two-thirds are appointed by an electoral college and the remainder nominated by the president.

Traditionally there were three levels of society in a system that was almost feudal: nobles, free men, and workers. These divisions vanished long ago, but those living on the high plateau (largely of Merina descent) have always considered themselves superior, while those in the coastal areas (côtiers) often feel deprived of power and education. When Madagascar gained its independence, the departing French ensured that the government was dominated by côtiers, and since then a conscious effort has been made to keep the Merina elite from power.

Madagascar is a member of the United Nations and the Organization of African Unity, and its current political environment is heavily influenced by foreign donors. There is a proposal by the World Bank and the International Monetary Fund (IMF) to create development zones around urban centers, which will result in further decentralization.

As president, Ratsiraka constantly pressed Madagascar's claims to various off-shore islands. Now that he is president again, these claims may be renewed.

THE FLAG OF MADAGASCAR

The national flag is simple in design. It has a white vertical section next to the hoist, one third of the flag in width. The remainder of the flag is filled with two equal horizontal stripes of red above green.

NATIONAL DEFENSE

Madagascar has no need of any extensive military force, so the small army of about 21,000 is used mainly for maintaining law and order, in conjunction with the police force of 7,500. Officially, there is compulsory military service for 18 months, but not all conscripts are called up. Most of those enrolled serve in the Service Civique, which mans development projects and helps to staff the state education system. There is reported to be an East German-trained secret police. The country's 500-strong navy includes 100 marines, and there is an air force with about 500 men. They operate combat aircraft that include fighters and helicopters from North

French troops were withdrawn in 1973 and the country now has its own armed forces, as well as a paramilitary force and secret police.

Korea, as well as Cessnas and transport planes. There are police stations but policemen are not often seen except at the airport. Police and army personnel wear camouflage and khaki uniforms and can be difficult to distinguish. The police tend to wear a blue kepi (as in France), while soldiers often have red or black berets. Since 1975 the army, navy, air force, and police have been incorporated into one body, the people's armed forces.

JUSTICE AND ADMINISTRATION

The judicial system is still modeled on that of France. The supreme court is in Antananarivo, and there is a court of appeal as well. There are eleven courts of first instance for civil and commercial cases, and ordinary criminal courts in most towns for criminal cases. Most judges and magistrates have had French training, but the traditional law of the Merina and other ethnic groups is taken into account by state magistrates when judging marriage, family, land, and inheritance cases.

The Malagasy system of law and justice is based on French codes and practices.

Local government includes the capital Antananarivo and six *faritany* ("FAR-i-TARN," or provinces)—Antsiranana, Fianarantsoa, Mahajanga, Toamasina, Tôlañaro, and Toliara—that are subdivided into prefectures and smaller counties where there may be localized community rule called *fokontany* ("FOOK-on-TARN"), or village social committees called *fokonolona* ("FOOK-on-o-LOON"). Each level is governed by an elected council. However, political change combined with a faltering economy has not provided reliable justice. There are suspicions that government

Francisque Ravony, a prime minister whose dismissal by President Albert Zafy led to the latter's impeachment on the grounds that the move was not constitutional.

officials starved of funds may turn a blind eye to smuggling or major fraud, and criminal gangs may actually enjoy protection from the police. As a result traditional methods of justice have not disappeared. There was a case in southeast Madagascar where peasants beheaded suspected thieves because they considered the local police and judiciary too inefficient and corrupt to execute justice.

TODAY'S CHANGING SITUATION

People no longer demonstrate against the government, as they did in 1991 to end the rule of President Didier Ratsiraka. They do not demonstrate because they are too busy surviving. The form of government has changed from authoritarian socialism to liberal democracy, but food is even harder to buy. The island is US$4 million in debt and cannot meet even the required interest payments. Industrial production has fallen and foreign investment declined drastically.

The survival of Madagascar's economy appears to rest on support from the outside world. The International Monetary Fund (IMF) has already laid down the details of a proposed austerity plan. Although this was supported by parliament, President Zafy rejected the proposal because he considered it too drastic on an island "where nearly half the children suffer retarded growth or acute malnutrition." This did not stop him from running up a bill of about US$10 million in April 1995 for a fleet of coastal patrol boats from Israel and training for 500 personal security guards.

POWER OF THE PRESIDENT

On August 19, 1992, a national referendum approved a new multiparty constitution that endorsed a unitary state (the Third Republic) and reduced the previous powers of the president. Under the new constitution, the president is elected by the vote of the people (for five years), while the prime minister is appointed by parliament and handles the day to day running of the country. However, the constitution names the president as the *ray aman-dreny*, a traditional title previously reserved for the king. President Albert Zafy insisted that this made him the moral authority for the nation and gave him a voice in the government.

In September 1995 a referendum was called to decide on this constitutional point: should the president have the power to appoint or dismiss the prime minister? (This power was previously entrusted to the National Assembly.) The Malagasy voters decided in favor of the president.

Prime Minister Francisque Ravony accused Zafy of illegal spending; Zafy then tried to fire Ravony. The move was blocked by parliament, and Zafy called a referendum to decide whether he had the right to dismiss the prime minister.

According to the constitution, the president is elected by the people and the prime minister is elected by parliament. Zafy won the referendum because his followers were afraid of any moves (like the IMF proposals) that might impose greater austerity. Zafy dismissed Ravony, but the legislature then impeached Zafy on the grounds that the referendum (and subsequent dismissal of the prime minister) were unconstitutional. The high court upheld parliament's impeachment of President Zafy for exceeding his powers. Zafy felt that he was the victim of a constitutional coup and vowed to return to office.

In November 1996 Madagascar held a presidential election with 17 presidential candidates including Zafy (the recently deposed president), Norbert Ratsirahonana (the incumbent prime minister), and Didier Ratsiraka (the previous president deposed by Zafy).

After the statutory two rounds of voting to determine the new president, the winner announced in January 1997 was Didier Ratsiraka, with 51% of the final vote. It is too soon to predict what effect this will have on the government of Madagascar.

ECONOMY

MADAGASCAR HAS BEEN RANKED by the World Bank as being among the 13 poorest countries in the world. The country is so deeply in debt that the International Monetary Fund (IMF) has given it the lowest possible rating, on a par with Zaire. The gross national product (GNP) is declining at around 1.7% per year, while the population is increasing by 3.1% annually. Madagascar has been looking for sources of money apart from the IMF. The country calls it parallel financing; the World Bank calls it money laundering. Whatever its efforts, Madagascar's treasury appears to be losing more money than it gains. The local currency has been devalued twice, in 1987 and 1991. Inflation is about 40% per year.

Opposite: **Wheat harvest for domestic consumption.**

Below: **Brickmaking using locally available clay, which is left in the sun to dry.**

ECONOMIC DECLINE

About 85% of the economically active population are farmers. Of these, 1.5 million farm on less than 5 acres (2 hectares) each. Before 1972, following the French colonial style, the government established producers' cooperatives that collected and processed most of the rice produced in the country at prices the peasants resented bitterly. The disquiet over this important crop led to domestic turbulence.

The post-1975 military regime attempted to introduce a "socialist paradise" and foreign firms were nationalized. The government also created state monopolies for import-export trading and the textile, cotton, and power industries were regulated. The economy soon declined. Exports fell, inflation rose, and foreign debt expanded

from $89 million (1970) to $250 million (1978) to $3.3 billion (1988). Imports nearly ceased for lack of foreign exchange needed to pay interest on the huge amounts that had been borrowed. Foreign investment declined to almost nothing, and the local currency (the Malagasy franc) was devalued. This hit hardest at the poorest people. The rural population struggled to survive, bartering with cattle and bags of coarse rice. By 1982 Madagascar was technically bankrupt.

In June 1990 France wrote off Madagascar's debt of 4 billion French francs in response to moves by President Didier Ratsiraka to allow a free-market economy. Since then, it has been providing an annual grant intended to educate farmers in the use of modern methods and machinery. South Africa showed interest in investing, and in September 1990, President F.W. de Klerk paid a visit to discuss "a new era of cooperation." But the economy did not strengthen sufficiently.

The IMF refused to consider any further loans unless Madagascar agreed to strict financial controls. State monopolies had to cease, and any state enterprise that could not pay its way was threatened with privatization.

Malagasy Bank of the Indian Ocean in Antananarivo.

TRADE AND INDUSTRY

The balance of trade is precariously unbalanced with imports (chemicals, machinery, and petroleum) being valued at almost double the exports (coffee, vanilla, sugar, and cloves). Nearly a third of all exports go to France, and 16% to the United States. Germany and Japan are other trading partners. Local industry is confined to rice mills and small factories, most in or around Antananarivo. Products include wood, paper pulp, cotton

fabric, fertilizer, oils, soap, sugar, cigarettes and tobacco, sisal rope, and mats. Mining production includes graphite, chromite, and mica. Other deposits include titanium ore, low-grade iron ore, low-grade coal, some nickel, and copper.

There is a variety of semiprecious stones, but nothing of great value. Offshore oil has been discovered, but not in sufficient quantity for commercial use. Toamasina, which has a deepwater harbor, is the main port. The oil refinery there has a production capacity of 12,000 barrels a day. Mahajanga is only accessible to small ships of shallow draft, but has considerable dhow traffic with the Comoros. Antsiranana (Diégo-Suarez) has one of the world's finest natural harbors and was once the French naval base, but is located far from the other main centers.

The Central Bank was formed in 1973. All commercial and banking institutes were nationalized in 1975, and privatized in 1988. The Malagasy Bank of the Indian Ocean was set up in September 1990 as part of a general bank privatization program. There are four central trade unions.

AGRICULTURE

Madagascar's economy is largely based on agriculture, which employs over 80% of the workforce and accounts for 75% of the exports. But because the countryside is mountainous, only 5% of the land is actually farmed. The main crops are rice, cassava, sugarcane, coffee, and vanilla. Overseas markets are unreliable so there is frequent overproduction and stockpiling. Rice is grown by 70% of the population and occupies about half the land under cultivation.

Sugarcane is farmed in plantations on the northwest and along the east coast. Cassava flourishes, and potatoes and yams are grown in the highlands. Corn does well only on the central plateau. Bananas are grown commercially on the east coast. Today many farmers are turning from the slow-growing crops such as vanilla and cloves to carrots, haricot beans, tomatoes, and other vegetables. Sisal plantations do well in the arid south, where factories discharge acidic green juice and the pure white sisal fibers are set out to dry. There is a small but steady production of local wine.

CATTLE AND FISHING

Zebu cattle, which presumably were introduced from Africa, are of great importance in Madagascar. The humped animals are a sign of wealth and are used for religious sacrifice, as well as for transportation and ploughing. Since it is considered more desirable to have a large number of thin cows than a smaller number of fat ones, the quality of local cattle remains poor, and this makes it difficult to breed them for meat consumption or export. Other domestic animals are sheep, goats, pigs, chickens, and a surprising number of camels. The Malagasy consider their wild animals such as the lemurs of little importance, although they are beginning to realize that tourists who show an interest in the creatures are a source of revenue.

There was a cotton boom between 1982 and 1986, but farmers who benefited from high export prices frittered away their new prosperity on endless rounds of festivities. They viewed it as a temporary windfall because the land on which the cotton was grown belonged to their ancestors, and the only thing of any real value to the ancestors was cattle.

Humped zebu cattle are found throughout the island.

43

Fishing is poorly developed, most of it being carried out by small traditional fishing communities using canoes called pirogues or small boats. Attempts have been made to stock rivers, lakes, and irrigated rice fields with breeding fish. The catch is used mainly for local consumption. Tourist hotels offer good quality seafood that includes tuna, plaice, lobster, crab, calamari, and prawns.

FORESTRY

Forests cover about a quarter of the land surface and contain many valuable hardwoods such as ebony, rosewood, and sandalwood, while gum, resins, and plants used for tanning, dyeing, and medicinal purposes are found in many places. However, the people need open land to cultivate rice and pasture their cattle, so they cut down the trees unceasingly.

Small boat fishers catch some 57,000 tons of fish each year.

VANILLA

Madagascar (together with Réunion and the Comoros islands) used to supply 80% of the world's vanilla. Most of the crop goes to the United States, where it is used by the ice cream industry and for the making of cola drinks (in which vanilla is an essential ingredient). However, exports have been threatened by overproduction and the creation of cheaper synthetic substitutes. In 1995 world exports of vanilla totaled 2,200 tons (2,000 tonnes) of which only 660 tons (600 tonnes), or 30%, came from Madagascar.

Vanilla is grown mostly on the hot, wet east coast where the vanilla orchids (originally from Mexico) are pollinated by hand. Nine months later, the seed pods will be 6 to 8 inches (15 to 20 cm) long. They are picked, blanched in vats of boiling water, then dried in the sun for about five months.

The resulting timber is used to supply 80% of household fuel, either in the form of logs or as charcoal, and the amount of forested land shrinks alarmingly every year. Only 30% of the wood and charcoal used for fuel is legally obtained; the rest is taken from supposedly protected areas. This deforestation allows the valuable topsoil to be washed away.

Although there are many narrow valleys with fast-flowing waterfalls, only a small number have been harnessed for hydroelectric power. Yet somehow these power stations are able to provide two-thirds of the country's electricity requirements. Thermal plants are another source of power. The possibility of a wider provision of bottled gas for cooking is being explored.

"They can see that the forest won't last forever."

—*Jean de Heaulme, owner of Berenty reserve, quoted in* National Geographic, *February 1987*

A woman carrying her child while planting rice in the ashes of a felled area of Ranomafana forest. This part of Madagascar is believed to be the home of the last 400 golden bamboo lemurs on earth.

"Madagascar, the world's best kept secret."

—*Tourist slogan thought up by Herizo Razafimahaleo, former Minister of Tourism and Industry*

TOURISM

Madagascar has much to offer tourists, and if the facilities and marketing were better regulated, the economy could see profound benefits. But the islands of Mauritius and the Seychelles lure visitors away with their better hotel and transportation arrangements. The real attractions of Madagascar are the unique flora and fauna and the friendliness of its people. Until roads, transportation services, and accommodation are improved, the majority of tourists will be those prepared to live rough.

Specially created reserves such as Périnet (east of Antananarivo) and Berenty or Kaleta Park (in the south) are proving of benefit to tourists and the local population. In the parks, wildlife can be viewed easily along walking trails, and lemurs will tumble out of the trees at the wave of a banana. They stand momentarily upright and then dance sideways, tail looped high, looking perpetually surprised. The parks also provide employment for wardens, guides, and domestic staff.

Trees and rare wildlife are being preserved—provided thieves do not gain access. This has happened at the Ankarafantsika forest reserve where intruders cut through a fence and stole two adult ploughshare tortoises and 73 hatchlings. Professional international smugglers then sell the endangered creatures for as much as US$3,000 each. Smart ecological tourism centers are being opened that offer an audiovisual explanation of the area, like the new one at Andohahela near Tôlañaro. The islands of Nosy Be and Nosy Boraha are accepting this challenge too, and are proving increasingly popular with overseas visitors.

Air Madagascar provides a domestic as well as international service, with flights being supplemented by those of several foreign airlines.

COMMUNICATION

No one can deny that the island's road transportation system is in a poor state. Only 10% of the roads are paved and most are full of potholes. The other roads are dirt tracks that are often impassable in the wet season. In theory, the Malagasy drive on the right-hand side of the road (as in the United States), but in fact they drive wherever there are any remaining fragments of hard surface. They drive their vehicles (most of them French) carefully, partly out of courtesy and partly because replacement parts are almost impossible to find. Most people travel by oxcart or *taxi-brousse* ("TAK-si-BROOSS," a minibus or pick-up truck).

For those who can afford it, flying is the favored way to travel. This is when the Malagasy wear their best clothes: ladies in fine dresses, and men in smart shirts. The national airline was originally called Mad Air until somebody thought it disrespectful. They renamed it Air Madagascar, so now it is known as "Air Mad." Air France and Russia's Aeroflot fly in from abroad. There is an international airports at Antananarivo, and most major towns around the island have a local airfield.

Much of the transportation system centers on Antananarivo and the facilities serve the slightly richer areas of the high plateau and the ports on the east coast. There are only four railway lines: three serve the capital, while the fourth links Fianarantsoa to the port of Manakara. Each has seldom more than one train a day. The line from Antananarivo to Toamasina is 235 miles (378 km) long. Built between 1901 and 1913, it is both a scenic wonder and a considerable engineering achievement. The Pangalanes Canal offers a waterway of lagoons linked with canals along

Madagascar has 532 miles (856 km) of railway track. The main line, which runs from Antananarivo to the east coast, was built by the French over a period of 12 years at the cost of hundreds of lives.

the east coast, but it is poorly maintained and only isolated stretches are usable. Communication between the capital (where decisions are made) and the villages (where the majority of people live) was improved during the Tsiranana regime by the arrival of the transistor radio. But the collapse of the road system by 1980 and the lack of cash to buy transistors, or even new batteries, has made communication of all types difficult. There is now an increased tendency towards village isolation.

The postal system does its best but is hardly reliable, while there are only about 25,000 telephones for the population of 13.5 million.

THE FUTURE

Madagascar's economic survival seems to be a desperate balance between preserving its forests and rare flora and fauna (thus attracting tourism and support from environmental organizations) and finding some way of stimulating its trade and capitalizing on its mineral resources.

Although the mining in Madagascar's southeastern coastal region may bring forced removals of people and possible desecration of sacred sites, the local people welcome anything that may mean a bit more money. At the time this book was written, there were rumors of a US$300 million project to dump toxic waste in Madagascar. The economy is desperate. Although a few diplomats and financiers drive through Antananarivo in elegant imported cars, much of the capital is home only to professional beggars and street children for whom there are no jobs and no schools.

An example of how the Malagasy will sell anything that anyone will buy.

MALAGASY

IT WOULD BE DIFFICULT to find a population so genuinely friendly, gentle, and courteous anywhere else in the world. There are exceptions, of course. Quick-profit merchants at popular tourist spots can be avaricious; street beggars in Antananarivo can be frighteningly persistent and even violent; and pickpockets thrive in the crowded town markets. These are reactions to urban poverty.

Above and opposite: **More than 95% of the population is Malagasy, with small communities of French, Comorian, Indian, Pakistani, and Chinese. The average life expectancy of Malagasy men is 55 years and women, 58 years.**

The real Malagasy are the people of the countryside and the villages. For many centuries before the arrival of the Europeans, they lived in geographical isolation, trying to strengthen the mutual bonds of kinship by marrying within the tribe. This was their protection against the outside, although they were also able to incorporate refugees from other groups.

People are hardworking and cheerful in spite of their poverty, although they are often wary of change. The markets are busy, with well-worn money changing hands after much bargaining. Those with cars drive with consideration for others, and radios are not played at a high volume, as in many African countries. Life seems relaxed, without too much of the pressures of 20th century living. There is a general attitude that "it is good to live here."

Nevertheless, in 1985, there were vicious riots that left 31 people dead. The riots were sparked by a government ban on *kung fu* clubs. Kung fu, a Chinese martial art, became a craze after Bruce Lee films from Hong Kong reached the country, giving rise to numerous clubs with members who belonged to the political right wing. When the president outlawed the clubs, the kung fu experts took to the streets where they found ready opposition to the government in the presidential youth movement, Tanora Tonga. The riots were eventually brought under control by government tanks.

ORIGINS

About 2,000 years ago Madagascar had no human inhabitants. No one is certain how the original settlers arrived, although Stone Age tools have been found and there are tales about a pygmy race occupying the center of the island. Tradition says that the first inhabitants were Malayo-Polynesians who crossed the Indian Ocean from Indonesia and Southeast Asia more than 1,500 years ago. Perhaps they were the Vazimba, a pastoral race who tended herds of cattle on the central plateau long before the Merina arrived.

Man descended from the Vazimba tribe standing among the limestone pinnacles known as tsingy.

"Scratch a Malagasy and the blood of many nations trickles out."

—*Local saying*

STATISTICS

Percentage of the population under 15: 50%
Life expectancy: 55 years for men and 58 years for women
Birth rate: 45.8 per 1,000
Deaths: 14 per 1,000 each year
Population density: 51 persons per square mile (20 per square km)
Urban population: 22%

Antananarivo was originally a Vazimba town called Analamangao, but nothing much is known about the place or people. Today, small groups descended from the Vazimba live in the rocky tsingy mazes where they are difficult to locate.

After the arrival of the original Vazimba, more settlers landed. In later years, those early inhabitants mixed with African slaves; Arab, Indian, and Portuguese traders; and French colonials to form the 18 official ethnic groups of the island today.

The modern inhabitants of Madagascar are called Malagasy (in English) or Malgache (in French); both are pronounced "mal-GASH." Although geographically close to Africa, Malagasy do not consider themselves to be Africans. Those living in the central highlands are mostly short and slim. They have straight black hair, light brown skin, dark eyes, and high cheekbones (indicative of their Malayan or Indonesian origins). Along the coast, people are often quite tall and much darker, with curly or even woolly hair, indicating their descent from later African immigrants.

ETHNIC GROUPS

Scholars have classified the people of Madagascar into 18 groups. These are not tribes but groups of mixed descent whose people tend to marry among their own kind. The rather vague boundaries of their lands are based on the traditional boundaries of ancient kingdoms.

Natural beauty treatments on the island are characteristically colorful.

Above: **Fishers sport bandannas of locally made, colorful cloth.**

Opposite: **Poor children in Antananarivo.**

The largest group is the Merina. They once ruled the island and now represent over a quarter of the population. The name means "elevated people," and they live on the high plateau around Antananarivo, where 95% of the people are Merina. There used to be three social groups: nobles, free men, and workers, but such divisions have been dispensed within democratic Madagascar. The *famadihana* ("fa-ma-DEE-an") ceremony of reburial originates with the Merina.

The next largest group is the Betsimisaraka, meaning "inseparable multitude" because the people were forged into one group from several smaller tribes. They live along the east coast where they have felt the influence of Europeans, particularly 18th century pirates who arrived by boat. Highly superstitious, they still believe in ghosts, mermaids, and little wild men from the forest that they refer to as *kalamoro* ("KAR-la-MOOR").

The Betsileo, or "invincibles," live on the central plateau south of Fianarantsoa. They are rice growers and woodcarvers. Merina and Betsileo are descended mainly from early Malayan and Indonesian immigrants.

GROWING POPULATION

Madagascar now has an ethnically diverse population of about 13.5 million with four fairly large non-Malagasy groups: French, Indo-Pakistani, Chinese, and Comorian. Before 1972 there were 50,000 French nationals, but by 1986 there were less than 15,000. The 10,000 Comorians are reportedly unpopular because of their wealth and a lifestyle that sets them apart socially. There used to be a larger community of Comorians, but after violent clashes and race riots, many of them were sent back to the Comoros in December 1977.

The population is growing rapidly, with a high concentration on the central plateau around Antananarivo, and lower density on the southeast coast. The western area is sparsely populated. About half of the population is under the age of 15, and three-quarters live in the countryside.

Government policy opposes any form of birth control, so the population is increasing at an average rate of 3.1% per year, one of the highest rates in the world. This means that the island's population is set to double every 25 years, which would indicate that the Malagasy are fast exceeding their country's capacity to

feed and employ them. The present population of around 13.5 million is estimated to rise to 16.1 million by the year 2000, and as much as 22.1 million by 2010.

The Malagasy believe that children are a gift from God and must be welcomed. It is regarded that the more children one has, the more one is blessed. It is quite normal for a family to have as many as eight or 10 children, and 14 is considered a lucky number.

DRESS

The all-purpose garment is the *lamba* ("LAM-ba"), a length of silk or cotton worn around the shoulders and often draped over the head. The way the lamba is draped indicates a woman's marital status, whether she is single, married, or widowed. If one end hangs down the right side of the body, it indicates mourning. Along the west coast women often wear sarongs, or loose skirts.

Although Madagascar is often considered to be part of the Africa continent, Malagasy are not Africans, but have a mixed ancestry of Indonesian, African, and other ethnic origins.

For the Merina, the lamba is usually white cotton draped across the left shoulder like a Roman toga. Women of other groups (such as the Sakalava and Antakarana) wear colorful cotton lambas that they use for carrying babies while shopping or working in the fields.

Men also wear lambas, either around the waist or tied in a knot on the shoulder. On special occasions they may wear the long *lamba mena* ("LAM-ba MAIN", meaning "red cloth" although it is seldom red) that indicates authority. The lamba mena also refers to the shroud used to wrap a dead body. Muslims wear the clothes indicated by Islamic tradition; men wear sober colors and usually a brimless cap, while married women are fully robed.

Nowadays, a separate garment is worn under the lamba. Women may wear a long robe, and men may wear jeans or shorts that are nearly always teamed with a hat, as it is seen as a sign of respectability. The Betsileo wear four-cornered hats, the Merina wear rice-straw hats, and the Bara wear cone-shaped hats. There are woven raffia hats for sale in every market, and the jaunty baseball cap has made its way to Madagascar.

Although boys may wear nothing more than a pair of shorts, girls and women dress modestly. Even if dressed in rags, girls cover the chest. All enjoy having their hair dressed. Some grease their hair with animal fat to make it shine. Girls tie their hair back with a colored ribbon. Most styles indicate happiness. When one is in mourning, the hair must be left to hang down, uncombed and untidy.

Boy wearing the lamba, the traditional Malagasy wrap.

LIFESTYLE

IN MADAGASCAR, AS ELSEWHERE in the world, there is a vast difference between the lifestyles of those with money and those without. The rich live as if the country were still a French colony; others only eat what they grow or can acquire by trade. An estimated 77% of Malagasy live in the country, growing rice, tending cattle, or doing something related to agriculture. Urban residents are less than a quarter of the population.

TOWN LIFE

The hilltops around Antananarivo are marked with

huge circles. These are the deep defensive ditches that once guarded fortified villages. Some had gates made of solid wheels of stone. Today's villagers do not need to defend themselves from other feuding groups and many have moved down the hills to be nearer to water supplies, but people are still wary of the outside world.

The biggest city in Madagascar is the capital, Antananarivo. Not only is it the center of government, education, and the economy, it is also a province in itself. The city spreads outward; houses are built on hills and ridges, and fields cover the floor of every valley. The inhabitants consider themselves city dwellers, even though some may plant rice and make sun-dried mud bricks. Theirs is a world of taxis and telephones, newspapers and schools, and freshly baked bread (long and thin in the French style) and machinery. Shops offer cameras and computers.

Richer families live in the Upper Town where the more expensive shops are. Narrow streets busy with traffic twist their way between blocks of shops and houses two or three stories high. On the lower slopes is a

Above: **Wealthier families live in the Upper Town in Antananarivo, where the houses have steep, angled roofs.**

Opposite: **The communal shower often acts as a meeting place for men of the community.**

sea of red walls, terracotta roof tiles, or rusty iron rooftops. An occasional white minaret and several church spires spring up in between.

Near the bright flowers and lawns of the Place de l'Indépendence stand most of the government buildings, including the impressive President's Palace, and Champion, the best supermarket in town with its array of food, clothes, and imported goods for those who have the money. The military, wearing scarlet berets, have sentry boxes with sloping stripes of white, green, and red.

The highest hill is crowned with the old Queen's Palace (called the Rova), which was gutted by a fire in 1995. There is also a miniature Greek temple that seems curiously out of place. The twisting road that plunges down the hillside passes tiny shops, women washing clothes on the pavement beside the communal tap, and a café called "Tarzan." Old shops are small and dark; behind a metal shutter, one man works with a sewing machine, while a woman weighs boxes of spices for sale.

Plastic, which does not rot and comes in bright colors, is replacing the soft, natural colors of wood in the towns. Life is crowded, dusty, shabby, and busy. Beggars tap on car windows with plastic mugs. Phone wires hang over the street and are draped in untidy festoons along the front of houses. Shuttered windows are protected with burglar bars, and barbed wire tops some walls. Yet those who live in the city are the lucky ones. They have access to the limited health resources, and most of their children go to school.

The Zoma market in Antananarivo has hundreds of stalls set up under huge, white umbrellas.

COUNTRY LIVING

Life in much of Madagascar can be summed up in one word—isolated. Whether people live beside lagoons, in the mountains, forests, or fields, the lack of roads and telephones makes communication difficult. The Malagasy are more concerned about the need to earn enough to live on. They may lead thin cattle to drying water holes, pick and sort vanilla pods, paddle dugout canoes in search of fish, or offer handfuls of nuts to potential customers.

Farmers, concerned with the year-long cycle of rice-growing, guide cattle round the fields to plough the mud with their hooves. They then plant rice seedlings, bending over flooded fields (a backbreaking job), tend to and weed the crop, and scythe the harvest. After that comes the work of pounding the rice in a wooden mortar. Most families grow only enough for their own needs, but often have to sell part of that to have some money.

Family selling yogurt, eggs, and goat meat by the roadside.

"The worst never happens in Madagascar."

—*Travel brochure*

61

The small community that lives beside Lake Anosy, a saltwater, inland lagoon near the southern tip of the island, is a typical small village. About 30 people live there in huts of wood and leaves. The men work in the nearby sisal plantation or fish the lake in pirogues made of baobab wood. Their nets, which are hung out on trees to dry, use stones for weights and carved baobab wood (which is very light) for floats.

The women search the tangled, spiny scrub for edible roots. Children play on the water's edge, careful not to touch the poisonous pink jellyfish. Most own one garment each. The older ones keep an eye on their few thin chickens, goats, and pigs.

What good timber remains in Madagascar is under constant attack. Woodcutters use old methods. A two-man team will cut a trunk into planks, one man guiding the saw on a high platform, the other below pulling and finding himself covered in sawdust. It is a hard way to earn a living.

Charcoal-burners use eucalyptus wood (the eucalyptus tree was introduced to replace the fast-disappearing forests), piling logs into stacks and leaving them to smoulder under a cover of turf sods for a week. The resulting sacks of charcoal may be the only source of income for the village.

In some communities the village is the woman's place and the forest is the man's; so it is a man's job to collect wood and a woman's task to use it for cooking.

Soap made from fat derived from the hump of zebu cattle.

CATTLE

Several hundred years ago, African humped-back cattle were introduced to Madagascar. Today, a herd of these cattle represents a walking bank account advertising the owner's wealth and respectability. One's importance in the local society is measured in cattle. If one manages to earn more money, one buys more cattle. Putting money in a bank is not a popular idea. Yet the cattle's significance extends beyond wealth. The well-being of

the herds stand for the continuing health and prosperity of the whole group of people to whom they belong. Fat humps show the cattle are in peak condition—but quantity is still considered more important than quality! Since cattle are such a sign of wealth, it is not surprising that there are cattle rustlers, especially in the savannah plains of the west and the dry south.

More than 80 words in the Malagasy language describe the people's beloved cattle and every part of their horns, hump, and hide. Each color means something different. White muzzles look like restricting nosebags, so it is said that the owner is unlikely to be prosperous. A dappled hide denotes uncertainty, whereas a hide of all one color—except black—indicates solidarity. Pure black means ruin, like black fields devastated by locusts. Black-and-white cattle seem safer.

Cattle are occasionally sacrificed to please the ancestors and are only sold if someone is very ill, or perhaps sacrificed to make that person well. After a funeral, horns will be put on the grave to show how many zebu were slaughtered for the feast and therefore how rich and important that person was.

FAMILY LIFE

The extended family has traditionally been the strength of Malagasy society. A family council that included the grandparents used to decide on children's upbringing, basing decisions on ideals such as family solidarity, respect for elders, and mutual help. However, much of this is changing, and many in Madagascar say: "Family life in the past is better than what it is today. The young were more respectful, and there was greater harmony." Today, the generation gap is being felt and the traditional family structure may not stand up to a more modern lifestyle.

Madagascar has an increasing number of single-parent families, particularly in the towns. The old ideal of having "seven boys and seven girls" is proving impossible. With a growing number of broken homes, children are sent out to work, while some are abused. Of 118 juvenile offenders held in custody in Antananarivo in 1996, 50% were abandoned as babies or left to fend for themselves.

Even when the family is intact, parents have to work and are often not around to teach their children the moral values of the past. This increasing lack of communication is the prime cause of delinquency. Children left to their own devices soon discover the world of drugs and petty crime. Many parents try to cope with this situation by adopting highly repressive and punitive attitudes, and this only leads to conflict within the home.

Three-generation Mala-gasy family.

> *"None of the roads is as good as it looks on the map."*
>
> —*Maureen Covell, in* Madagascar: Politics, Economics & Society

DAILY SURVIVAL

Beggars are everywhere; children sleep in doorways, while others sift through garbage heaps. To the Western world, such poverty is disturbing. Madagascar is not proud of it but life has to go on.

In parts of the desert-dry countryside, which receives no rain for seven or eight months, survival is a skill for both people and plants. Spiky plants and succulents have found a way to live and likewise, the humans have learned to survive as well. There seems hardly anywhere to live or anything to live on, and for many months of the year, it may be too hot to work. Still, people carry firewood, water, vegetables, logs, and bulging sacks of rice in the hope of making a sale whenever they can. They do the washing in the river, but it does not make much difference—clothes are ragged and stained with dirt and sweat anyway.

Poverty can create desperation. Whenever a tourist arrives, children swarm out from nowhere in search of candy, fruit, pens, or money. Foreigners sometimes find themselves mobbed by beggars, all uneducated, homeless, and desperately poor, with no chance of employment and no help from the government.

TRANSPORTATION PROBLEMS

"Madagascar is not an island but an archipelago" is a local saying that emphasizes the diversity of the people and the poor means of communication. As part of their defense strategy, several precolonial

Washing clothes in the river is very much a part of rural life.

65

kingdoms refused to build roads. Even today it seems as if the Malagasy do not want better roads because that may bring an invasion of people. Most tracks are made of dirt or mud and are almost unusable after it rains. One favored Malagasy expression is *mandrevou* ("MAND-dr-FOH"), which means "bottomless mud." The few paved roads are full of potholes and road markings are unknown. Serious travelers go by air or go port-hopping around the coast by boat.

Street traffic may consist of carts pulled by two zebu oxen roped to a wooden yoke, ramshackle bicycles, or sometimes a car or van. But there are two vehicles that are special to Madagascar. The first is the *pousse-pousse* ("POOSS-POOSS," meaning "push-push"), a cart for passengers or goods, pulled by one man. It is similar to the Chinese rickshaw. Antsirabe is Madagascar's pousse-pousse capital, where Chinese laborers brought in to work on the railways probably introduced the idea.

The other special vehicle is called a *taxi-brousse*, usually a minibus or pick-up truck. Almost any vehicle will serve the purpose, although most

are minibuses. The taxi-brousse service is part of the Malagasy lifestyle. In theory, it plys between towns according to a timetable, but in fact, it leaves only when there are enough people to make the trip worthwhile. The more people who squeeze in, the better in terms of income for the driver.

Crowded pick-up truck providing a taxi service in Morondava. Some travel long distances and carry farm animals as well as people.

BIRTH

The birth of a baby is a time for rejoicing because God is seen to have been generous. Many children are given a Christian name in church, as well as a traditional Malagasy name. The time of day at which that baby is born is considered important and is part of the child's fortune, or *vintana* ("vin-TARN"). A baby born at dawn is destined to be an industrious and good worker, one born at midday may rise in fortune like the sun, and one born in afternoon sunlight should find golden riches. However, if the birth process is slow and at a time when the sun is setting, then life's fortunes may fade away.

MARRIAGE

Marriage is a celebration of the natural life process of choosing a partner and starting a family. Christians celebrate with Western-style ceremonies; others, who adhere to the older customs, still negotiate a bride price in cattle, money, and gifts. These are meant to go to the prospective bride to help her set up her new home, but fathers play a strong role in negotiations and sometimes keep part of the money.

In exchange for these gifts, including the man's promise to build her a house, the woman is expected to provide the necessary household goods, including bedding and cooking pots. A trial marriage is encouraged. The minimum legal age for marriage is 17 for boys and 15 for girls. Brides are sometimes still in school and attend class with babies strapped to their backs.

Wedding procession in which a relative carries a suitcase containing the bride and groom's belongings.

OFF TO MARKET

Every day is market day, but Friday is special. The huge area in Antananarivo used for market trading is called the *Zoma* ("ZOO-mah"), meaning "Friday." Here, under white umbrellas or draped awnings, all sorts of things are for sale: fruit, vegetables, eggs, dried fish, pungent spices, caged birds, used shoes, second-hand clothes, cassette tapes, sacks of charcoal, kitchen implements, and cast-iron cooking pots. Here, too, can be found persuasive salesmen, beggars, and pickpockets.

In the smaller towns, the goods are less exotic. People go to market to haggle for the necessities of life: rice, roots, vegetables, salt, paraffin, candles, plastic bowls, and water cans—some are filled with *toaka gasy* ("TOH-ka GASH"), the illegal homemade rum. The unit of measure is the *kapoka* ("kar-POOK"), the amount of rice (or dry goods) that will fill an empty, condensed milk can. Hopeful buyers sort through boxes of old pieces of machinery, bolts, wrenches, and rusting bicycle parts. Traders wander with trays of fruit, flowers, footballs, or baskets of shells.

The equivalent of a fastfood stall is one selling banana fritters, spicy triangular *sambos* ("SAM-bohs," or samosas), or slices of coconut.

People make a living selling fruit and vegetables, as well as all sorts of recycled goods.

69

Protestant and Roman Catholic missions have been providing education in Madagascar since the 19th century, although there are now government schools at all levels as well.

EDUCATION

School is compulsory for all children from age 6 to 14. The University of Madagascar's main campus is in Antananarivo, and there are five university centers in the other provincial capitals, as well as technical institutes, teacher-training colleges, and four agricultural schools. Enrollment in universities has increased rapidly in recent years. There are about 5,000 literacy centers throughout the country staffed by people doing such work for their national service, or by workers of nongovernmental organizations. Although government statistics claim that 80% of students attend school, the average literacy rate in the country may be as low as 40%. Private schools (such as those run by the Alliance Française) play a significant role in the education system.

As with so much else in Madagascar, there is a huge difference between educational opportunities in and around the capital and what happens in the rest of the country. In Antananarivo most children between age 6 and

WILDLIFE APPRECIATION IN SCHOOLS

In 1987 the government of Madagascar asked the World Wildlife Fund (WWF) to help develop an environmental curriculum and produce teaching materials for the country's primary schools. Primary and secondary teachers have learned how to use these materials and are now integrating environmental subjects into the classroom. Schools lead the way in spreading a message of tree-planting and the dangers caused by cutting down the forests. The WWF sponsors the publication of *Vintsy* (meaning "kingfisher"), a bimonthly ecology magazine for secondary schools.

11 attend school, but in a coastal town like Morondava, less than a third do so. Government publications quote an average of 38 students per teacher at the elementary level in the 13,600 schools around the country. Yet a secondary school teacher admits he has one class of 80 pupils, making it difficult to teach effectively.

In the cool of the early morning children make their way to school. School hours are from 7 a.m. to 10 a.m. and from 3 p.m. to 5 p.m., with a long midday rest because of the high temperatures. Recently, attempts have been made to incorporate farming skills, basic hygiene, and nutrition into the primary curriculum. All instructions are given in French and most textbooks come from France. In their sixth year, 13-year-old children will learn conversational English, a skill that may be the key to a better job.

HEALTHY LIVING

Between 1975 and 1984 the government expanded the number of trained health service personnel from 3,900 to 8,200 as part of a policy aimed at putting a health facility

Children at the gates of a private school.

within 6 miles (10 km) of every Malagasy family. The economy's poor performance has necessitated cuts in this service, and it is estimated that only 65% of the population have access to local health care. Malnutrition is common, and the population continues to increase in spite of a high infant mortality rate of 95 per 1,000 live births.

Parasitic diseases are hard to control because the irrigated rice fields and the streams that feed them often provide fertile breeding grounds for disease-carrying pests. Only a third of the population have access to safe water. Malaria has returned to pose an even greater menace since the decision in 1984 to stop the provision of chloroquine to schoolchildren. The United Nations Children's Fund has since helped to launch an immunization program, but hygiene is often lacking, with beaches and roadsides commonly used as lavatories.

There are about 750 hospitals in the country (although the term includes health centers), providing on average one hospital bed for every 586 people. Most hospitals are in the towns, with some rural hospitals and clinics run by Christian missions. There are approximately 1,200 doctors, 100 dentists, and 90 pharmacists, and 4.2% of the national budget is spent on medical care. Health insurance and other social benefits are available to the better-paid workers. Bottles of medicine are available on the black

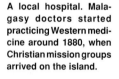

A local hospital. Malagasy doctors started practicing Western medicine around 1880, when Christian mission groups arrived on the island.

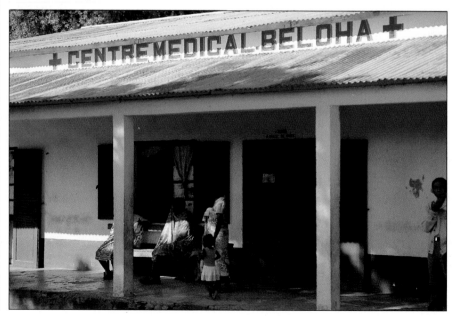

market, but these are probably sold by the families of patients who were given the medicine, but never took it. Recently the Antananarivo municipality and the international organization Médecins sans Frontières have made free medical care available for Antananarivo's street children.

In the countryside western medicine remains expensive and difficult to obtain. Many people still trust in traditional medicine, handed down through the generations. The rainforests are full of medicinal plants used for herbal treatment. The *raraha* plant, for example, has anesthetic qualities and is used to ease sore gums and toothache. People in the country believe that illness may have more than a physical cause and that a healer does not cure the illness alone, but the whole person. The traditional healer is called the *ombiasy* ("om-bi-ASH") and works by means of invocations or charms with perhaps an animal sacrifice.

Lack of proper sanitary facilities contributes to the spread of disease.

RELIGION

THE MALAGASY REGARD THEIR COUNTRY as the sacred land of their ancestors, who remain its rightful owners. Most of them believe in one God, either in a traditional or Christian sense. Many claim to go to church, but that does not stop them from making sacrifices to their ancestors. Christianity is practiced alongside traditional beliefs; it has not taken their place.

ORGANIZED RELIGION

The Christian faith has existed in Madagascar ever since King Radama I encouraged missionaries to start work in the early 19th century. Over a period of 15 years, they opened schools and chapels, produced the first dictionary of the Malagasy language, translated the Bible into Malagasy, and converted many to Christianity. The London Missionary Society

Left: **Missionaries run European-style ministries in a country where Christianity coexists with the cult of ancestor worship.**

Opposite: **A tribal tomb of the Mahafaly people in southern Madagascar. Traditional Malagasy pay tribute to their dead with totem-like structures adorned with the skulls and horns of cattle sacrificed in funeral rites.**

brought Protestant Christianity, but as French influence increased, so did Catholicism. The Protestant churches are mainly in the highlands, with the more numerous Roman Catholics mostly near the coast.

Radama's widow was called the Murderous One; in the 1840s she prohibited Christian practices, killed those who disobeyed, and forced missionaries to leave. Stonebuilt churches in Antananarivo stand in memory of Madagascar's first Christian martyrs. One inscription reads, "Erected by the London Missionary Society in memory of 12 individuals who died in or near Madagascar in endeavoring to introduce on the island the blessings of civilization and the knowledge of the glorious gospel of the Blessed God." About 28% of the population is Roman Catholic, 22% Protestant, and 5% Muslim. The rest of the population practice traditional beliefs.

TRADITIONAL WORSHIP AND DESTINY

The earliest Malagasy believed in a supreme being as well as secondary deities or spirits that haunted waters, trees, and stones. They also respected creatures such as snakes, crocodiles, and lemurs, and held that humans have spirits that do not die after bodily death.

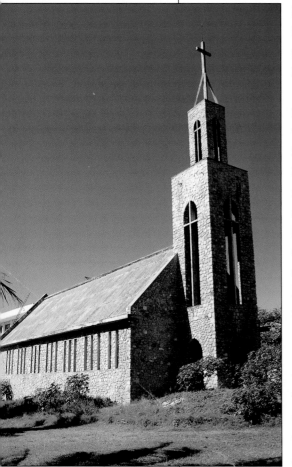

A church at Tôlañaro, formerly occupied by the French. Much of the singing of Christian hymns is delivered in the distinctive Malagasy style.

Even today, the people believe strongly in their ancestors' power to influence disasters (such as famine, drought, and cyclones), as well as happiness, prosperity, and luck. The dead are not regarded as having departed but are believed to remain with the family and play as important

THE BEGINNING OF MANKIND

This is the Malagasy version of how God put men on the earth. The god Andriananahary looked down from the heavens on to a sunbaked, empty island. He wondered about the place. Could anyone survive there? Somebody would have to go and find out.

Andriananahary called his son, Atokoloinona, who was playing among the clouds. He explained the task: to go down to the earth and see what it was like. So Atokoloinona floated down to the hot, dry land and looked around him. He was pleased to be given this mission and keen to return with a good report. But all round him was rock and sand. There were no plants, trees, or water, and the ground burned his feet. Sadly, he realized that he had to tell his father that nothing would be able to live on the earth.

So he tried to launch himself from the top of a sand dune, but something was very wrong. He could not fly. The sun was drying him up. In desperation, Atokoloinona dug a hole deep in the sand and hid himself. Night fell and there was no sign of his son. Andriananahary became worried. When sky and earth remained empty the next morning, he sent his servants to earth to search everywhere. They scurried in all directions but could find no trace of Atokoloinona. Before long the heat began to affect them too. They cracked and withered like dry leaves.

The god Andriananahary stretched out his hand and there came thunder, lightning, and torrential rain. As the water reached the earth, the desert turned green and became a paradise. So the servants were glad. They stayed and became mortal men. But Andriananahary's son was never seen again. This old story helps to explain why the Malagasy consider that the ground itself is sacred and everything that grows is a gift from God.

a role as they did when they were alive. Thus they must be revered, consulted, pleased, and asked to bestow good fortune on the family. A family may throw a party in honor of an ancestor. Each tribe has its own beliefs, and practices different ways of burying their dead. An ancestor's soul can die if it is left out of the thoughts of its relatives. At village gatherings people ask their ancestors' permission to hold the meeting. Nobody is thought to be "dead and gone."

From such customs arises the idea of personal fate or destiny (vintana) and the conviction that certain actions are forbidden (fady) because they bring bad luck. Belief in vintana is particularly strong in the coastal areas exposed to Islamic influence. They believe there are certain times of high and low fortune, often foretold in the stars according to the moment of one's birth. So there are good or bad vintana periods. By choosing the "best times" for birth, circumcision, marriage, or burial, people can prevent

Above: **Steps up the sacred hill of Ambohimanga are lined with street vendors selling kebab and other foods.**

Opposite: **A tomb carving of a human form shows a mix of tribal and Christian influences.**

accident, illness, and trouble. The choice of a marriage partner is complicated by vintana. Every person is said to represent one of the basic elements of water, fire, wind, or hill. Wind cannot marry hill; fire can marry wind, but if fire marries water the fire will be put out.

Days of the week have their own vintana. Monday can bring sorrow but is a good day for purification ceremonies; Tuesday is an unreliable day, bad for important agreements but good for travel and having fun; and Wednesday is "the day of poor return," so if one plants on that day there will be a poor harvest and, even more alarming, if one goes traveling one may not come back. Thursday is the holiest day of the week, so no one can work in the fields on that day, but it is acceptable for most sacred rites except burial; Friday (associated with nobility) is a good day; and Saturday and Sunday are unthreatening days when one can work safely. The village ombiasy chooses suitable days for sowing, harvesting, marriage, and burial. There are good times of day too. Sunrise is usually a fortunate time to begin something, while the middle of the night is to be avoided.

Those who are very poor find that things seem to go wrong all the time, and many want their bad luck to be turned into good luck. The Malagasy believe strongly in luck. When something goes wrong, they believe they have offended an ancestor in some way. Some people might call the

Malagasy superstitious, but for them, the fady rules and taboos are simply part of daily life, varying from tribe to tribe and one village to another.

Many other superstitions prevail as well. In Antananarivo, for example, people believe that evil spirits cannot climb steps, so buildings have many flights of steps to deter the spirits. Almost everywhere in Madagascar people are sure that evil lurks at night, so homes are built without chimneys in case some spirit should enter there, and windows are shuttered and doors bolted securely after dark.

FUNERALS AND TOMBS

Reverence for one's ancestors means that one must give them an impressive farewell ceremony and a suitable dwelling place. Death is not normally a time for mourning. Without the blessing of the ancestors, nothing can go well. The Malagasy have a saying, "A house is for a lifetime; a tomb is for eternity." In any case, the word "dead" is not used; instead, the deceased has been "loosened" or "untied."

The body is washed and covered with a white cloth. It is usually kept in the house for a few days while mourners gather. They will bring with them gifts of money that can only be used to pay for funeral expenses—it is fady to use it for any other purpose. A tribal elder's funeral may be a noisy affair going on all night, for some believe that they can banish death by wailing and drumming. The body is wrapped in an expensive shroud

and buried, with the head facing east and the feet facing west, in whatever style is used in that area. In the west and on the plateau, children do not inherit their father's cattle. When he dies, his herd of cattle is slaughtered and their horns displayed on the tomb to show his importance.

All Malagasy names have meanings. When a person dies, relatives choose a new name for the deceased that highlights his or her good qualities—for example, "He who made work look easy" or "The woman who did her duty." Any living relative who has the same name as the deceased's newly acquired one must change his or her name. It is fady to use the same name. In Sakavala

Tomb decoration showing a man with his beloved cattle.

custom, the widow in mourning dresses in old clothes and remains in the house. She does not speak to anyone except for close relatives. When the period of mourning (which can be several weeks) is over, she will dress in clean clothes, come out of the house and speak to people as a sign of returning to the normal world.

Throughout the island, each tribe handles funerals and burial rites in its own way. The common factor is that all want their tombs to be more permanent than their houses. Those tombs might be in the shape of stone mausoleums, cave-tombs, underground chambers with stone shelves, or painted walled enclosures. Other structures are sometimes used in place of tombs: long stone lines with crosses mounted on them, carved wooden totem poles in the shape of people and animals, or obelisks marked only

TURNING OF THE BONES

Few customs are stranger than that of *famadihana* ("fa-ma-DEE-an"). It is practiced mainly by the Merina people on the high plateau and is regarded as a duty that the living owes to the deceased. This involves opening the tomb, removing the old shroud (called a lamba), washing and rewrapping the body in a fine new silk shroud, and then replacing it reverently. Since the ancestors are not thought to have departed and their spirits are very much alive, they must be welcomed, talked to, and entertained. What is important is to show that they have not been forgotten, and family members may even hug them or dance with them. Tears will not please the deceased.

The famadihana can last for a day or two, which means that the family will have to hire a band, employ an ombiasy, sacrifice cattle, and pay for food and refreshments. Even devout Christians may take part. Depending on the family's wealth, the ceremony is held every three, five, or seven years, but only during the winter months.

Christian churches may frown on famadihana but have not attempted to forbid it because the custom is so deeply rooted in the lifestyle of the people. It is the source of their loyalty to their hometown or village, signifies their attachment to their tribal group, and demonstrates their respect for older people and the deceased. There are signs, however, that the practice is waning, partly because it is not in keeping with church custom, but mainly because of its cost.

with a name (in which case the burial place is elsewhere, its location kept secret). The most elaborate tombs are those constructed by the Mahafaly people in the south, using intricately carved upright pillars with sculptures and inscriptions. Sorrow belongs on the "cold" south side of a village, so tombs are usually sited there and built only at night. The shadow of a tomb must not touch the homes of the living.

LANGUAGE

MADAGASCAR'S LANGUAGE, MALAGASY ("mal-GASH"), is almost as unique as its rare lemurs, chameleons, and orchids. Related to the Malayo-Polynesian family of languages spoken in the Malay Peninsula, with the addition of some words from Africa and Arabia, Malagasy is a blend of Asia and Africa, with features not found anywhere else in the world.

GROWTH OF A LANGUAGE

In a country where the skills of reading and writing are still not universal, the spoken word remains highly important. The Malagasy language derived from Indonesia is remarkably uniform throughout the island, with very few regional variations.

Above and opposite: **French, an official language, is also the medium of instruction in schools.**

The Antaimoro were the first people in Madagascar to adopt writing. Their holy men traveled widely throughout the country, adding an Islamic influence to the local language. Malagasy still uses Arabic-derived names for days of the week. It also contains adopted words from French, English, and other tongues. Because the first missionaries were British, Malagasy words relating to religion, education, or anything literary often have an English base, whereas anything to do with food or drink tends toward French, and other words dealing with cattle and domestic animals come from the Kiswahili spoken in Africa.

The use of playful language is introduced in the early years, as children learn the symbolic importance of question and answer through the basic word game of riddling. Through metaphor, they find that language is ambiguous. Here are some of their riddles:

"God's stick has water in its stomach" (sugarcane).

"Five men with round hats" (fingers).

"White chicks filling a hole" (teeth in mouth).

The skill of speaking in public, called *kabary* ("ka-BAHR"), is still very much a part of Malagasy culture. Village elders can speak for hours, using witty double meanings and complicated proverbs. It is a traditional skill, used especially at weddings and funerals, even if the younger folk do not have much time for it now. They enjoy using more words than may seem necessary. When asked how far away a particular place is, a Malagasy might answer, "A person walking fairly fast will probably reach there in the time it takes to cook a pot of rice."

Malagasy is rich in poetic images and its isolation from its spoken roots in Southeast Asia has helped it evolve into a unique language.

WRITTEN RECORDS

In European literature, the earliest mention of Madagascar seems to have been made by Marco Polo in the 13th century. He wrote, "You must know that this island is one of the biggest and best in the whole world"—although he may have confused it with Mogadishu in Somalia because one of the spelling forms that he used was Mogdaxo.

Other theories on the meaning of that name are "Island of Ghosts" or "Island of Ancestors." Visiting Arabs called Madagascar "The Island of the Moon." The Malagasy themselves use terms such as "The Great Island," "The Red Island," or "The Happy Island."

TOMBOLA
SEKOLIN'NY MISIONA KATOLIKA ISOTRY
TIRAGE 8 JUILLET 1972
— DATE IRREVOCABLE —
VIDIN-KARATRA 50 FMG
GROS LOTS

MAFONJA

Among Marco Polo's mixture of reported truths and fictions was the mention of a giant bird that he called a gryphon and that the islanders called *rukhs*. A giant bird also appears in the *Arabian Nights*, where Sinbad the Sailor refers to a *roc* that can "truss elephants in its talons." Could this have been Madagascar's now extinct elephant bird?

Radama I, who was given the title of "king" by Sir Robert Farquhar, British governor of Mauritius, sent out a request for missionaries to help with Madagascar's education and development. Two of those sent by the London Missionary Society were Welshmen David Jones and David Griffiths. With help from the king, they set about recording the Malagasy language in the European (Latin) alphabet. The first school was set up, and by 1835 the Bible was printed in Malagasy. However, it remains a language that is spoken rather than written.

There are numerous dialects and local variations of Malagasy, but they are all mutually intelligible.

LANGUAGE DILEMMA

The problem so often encountered in developing countries is that of whether to teach children in their mother tongue or a First World language. In 1972 Malagasy replaced French as the medium of instruction in schools in the hope of making education more accessible to all. But to be literate in a language used only on one island in the world does not help international communications. So in 1986 French was reintroduced in secondary schools. It is now the language of instruction in all schools and is used for literary, business, and administrative purposes. It is functional but not over-popular with the people; a qualified schoolmaster may teach in French and English, yet think in Malagasy.

Malagasy remains the spoken language throughout the island. English, which used to be spoken only to tourists, is now seen as desirable for business reasons. Among the many notices posted in Malagasy outside a church, which acts as a village's social center, there may be a notice in French announcing the activities of the local "English Club"—offering villagers the opportunity to speak English "without hesitation" and be a "man of affairs or tourist guide." The newspaper *Midi Monde* has a page in English, with a glossary of "new words," while *L'Express* has a cartoon strip in French on Indian Ocean pirates. Both newspapers are mainly in French, as indicated by their names, but have columns in Malagasy.

In Antananarivo French is spoken as often as Malagasy. In rural areas, however, it may be resented as a colonial language, so people use Malagasy at home, French in school, and English on the beer bottles—labeled Three Horses Beer, even though there are very few horses in Madagascar.

Three Horses Beer, a local brew, varies from the written and spoken trend with its English name.

Since Madagascar gained its independence from France, many towns have reverted to their original names. Here are some of the old Malagasy and newer French names:

Malagasy	French
Mahajanga	Majunga
Antsiranana	Diégo-Suarez
Nosy Boraha	Sainte Marie
Toamasina	Tamatave
Toliara	Tuléar
Tôlañaro	Fort Dauphin

Most people seem happy enough that the island itself is still called Madagascar, although in the Malagasy language it is Madagasikara.

Signboards of seaside hotels in French.

HOW TO SAY THE WORDS

The Malagasy alphabet has 21 letters. The following letters are not used: *c, q, u, w,* and *x; c* is replaced by *s* or *k,* and *x* with *ks.* The letter *o* is usually pronounced like *oo,* so *veloma* (goodbye) is pronounced "ve-LOOM." The stress is usually on the penultimate syllable, although vowels that come at the end of a word are sometimes not pronounced at all. For example, the *sifaka* lemur is pronounced "SHE-fak." A general rule seems to be, "swallow as many syllables as you can and drop the last one." Sometimes the way one says a word changes its meaning—*tanana* ("TAN-an-a") means "hand," but *tanána* (written with an accent and pronounced "ta-NA-na") means "town." In general, the Malagasy language has no accents. Words with diacritics, or accent marks, are of French origin.

Malagasy is a poetic language. For example, the term for the early hours of the morning is translated "when the wild cat washes itself." Names of people and places also have meanings. Antananarivo, the capital, means "city of the thousand" because it is said that a thousand warriors originally guarded it. Words are often joined together (as in Welsh or German) to create long personal and place names. For example, people think nothing of pronouncing the name of the island's most famous king, Andrianimponi-merinatsimitoviaminandriampanjaka, without drawing a breath.

GREETINGS

Greeting a friend is a serious affair and must not be hurried. The traditional Malagasy greeting is to take an offered hand between one's own hands. Those who are more modern copy the French fashion, kissing three times on alternate cheeks, but they like to shake hands too.

Salama ("sal-AHM"), a greeting in some coastal regions, is a variation on the Arabic *salaam*. The more common greeting is *manao ahaona* ("mano OHN"). Europeans are not called "white" because the color white is considered offensive; "white" refers to all that is ugly and of low quality, and an unreliable person is one who speaks "white words." So visitors are called *vazaha* ("va-ZAH"), or foreigner. The Malagasy are extremely courteous and do not speak too loudly. They do not speak lightly of old people or death.

> *"The Malagasy language is a joy to listen to but a torment to pronounce."*
>
> —*Dervla Murphy, in* Muddling Through in Madagascar

SOME COMMON WORDS

Hello	*Manao ahoana* ("mano OHN")
What news	*?nona no vaovao?* ("EE-nan vow-vow")
No news	*Tsy misy* ("tsee MEESS")
Please/Excuse me	*Aza fady* ("a-za FAAD")
Thank you	*Misaotra* ("mis-OW-tr")
Goodbye	*Veloma* ("ve-LOOM")

ARTS

THE MALAGASY ARE CLOSE TO NATURE. The artist, sculptor, wood-carver, or painter does not try to create an imitation of the world around him. His world is one in which a creator God has given the spirit of life to everything—humans, animals, plants, and stones alike. Even the deceased retain their spirit. So any work of art must be so beautiful that it pleases the spirit for whom it is intended, and perhaps attracts the spirit to live in or feel associated with it. Even music is often something created out of emotion generated by a special moment.

For most poor people, an object's worth or beauty is judged by its usefulness. So weavers make cloth to wear or hats for shade; embroiderers make tablecloths or collars; and woodcarvers make tomb adornments in stone or wood. Such tomb adornments acquire a sacred quality as well.

Left: **Merina and Betsileo women are adept at French-style sewing and embroidery.**

Opposite: **Woman selling replicas of the extinct elephant bird's egg.**

Madagascar's well-established printing industry —introduced in the 1820s by the London Missionary Society—supports the production of written literature in Malagasy, including poetry, scholarly works, and contemporary writings.

In the capital city of Antananarivo, there are museums of history, art, and archeology, as well as the National Library. The Albert Camus Cultural Center is used for many concerts and film shows, while branches of the Alliance Française in Antananarivo and around the country stage cultural events. There is national pride in the country's cultural history. The restoration of the burned-out Queen's Palace in Antananarivo, for example, has drawn support from several provincial councils, notably those of Toliara and Toamasina, as well as that of the capital itself. There is also generous support from the German government.

Tsimbazaza Zoo includes displays of dinosaur bones and elephant bird eggs, an ethnographic museum showcases the cultures and peoples of the land, and there is a terrarium of indigenous reptiles.

LITERATURE

The most popular use of language in Madagascar is oral; there is a long tradition of oratory, known as kabary, that includes speechmaking and storytelling. Originating with the tribal council of elders, this skill has been extended from political polemic to sheer entertainment. A skilled speaker spins a web around his subject, referring to it in clever metaphors and intricate proverbs and references, never coming directly to the point, to the delight of his audience.

Proverbs are rich and popular, combining wisdom and wit. For example:

"You can trap an ox by its horns and a man by his words."

"The man who refuses to buy a lid for the pot will eat badly cooked rice."

"If you are only a dungbeetle, don't try to move mountains."

LEGENDS

Legends feature strongly in Madagascar's oral tradition. One of the many favorite tales is that of the voronjaza bird (or sickle-billed vanga).

The story is set in a time of raiding pirates and slave traders, when a mother and her child took refuge in the thick forest. Raiders who were close by heard a baby crying and headed toward the sound, laughing cruelly and anticipating with delight what they would find. Then they heard the sound again, but at that moment the voronjaza hopped onto the branch of a tree and gave its call, which sounded just like the cry of a newborn baby. The pirates cursed the fact that they had been fooled by a bird and sailed away.

The mother, however, knew that the bird had saved her child's life, for the first wail from her baby had been real enough. So the voronjaza remains honored, and to this day it is fady to kill a voronjaza.

When writing was first introduced to Madagascar by the Antaimoro people who settled near the Matitane River in the southeast, it seemed magical and full of power. Their religious texts were held in great awe, and their ability to write gave them power and prestige throughout the land. These writings, known as *Sorabé*, contained prayers, magic formulas, genealogies, memorable events, and legends. The Malagasy words were written on paper made from bark and with ink extracted from the gum tree, and in an Arabic script so ancient that no one can decipher it today. This was the only form of writing in Madagascar until the first missionaries arrived. Unfortunately, they considered the Sorabé books to be examples of witchcraft and burned all those they could find.

There is little famous Malagasy writing, apart from the patriotic poetry of Jean-Joseph Rabearivelo in the 1940s. The town of Fianarantsoa, an ancient center of learning, has gained a name as the island's literary capital. A number of writers have published their works there, of which Emilson D. Andriamalala is the best known. However, there is a traditional style of love poetry perfected by the Merina called *hainteny* ("HAY-ten-i").

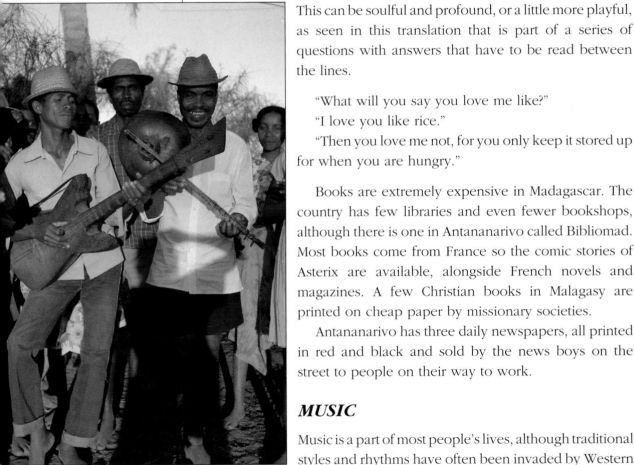

Above: The man at right is carrying a gourd resonator with two sets of strings.

Opposite: A traditional musician holds flute-like instruments.

This can be soulful and profound, or a little more playful, as seen in this translation that is part of a series of questions with answers that have to be read between the lines.

"What will you say you love me like?"

"I love you like rice."

"Then you love me not, for you only keep it stored up for when you are hungry."

Books are extremely expensive in Madagascar. The country has few libraries and even fewer bookshops, although there is one in Antananarivo called Bibliomad. Most books come from France so the comic stories of Asterix are available, alongside French novels and magazines. A few Christian books in Malagasy are printed on cheap paper by missionary societies.

Antananarivo has three daily newspapers, all printed in red and black and sold by the news boys on the street to people on their way to work.

MUSIC

Music is a part of most people's lives, although traditional styles and rhythms have often been invaded by Western pop music. The Malagasy, especially the men, like singing in harmony. Many of the songs are church hymns because Malagasy social life often centers around the church, but the people sing folk songs too.

Local instruments include a cone-shaped drum of Indonesian origin and the *valiba* ("va-LEE-b"). This is similar to a zither, with 21 or more

HIRA GASY

This traditional entertainment (pronounced "HEE-ra GASH") is the Sunday showpiece of Antananarivo, although traveling groups also tour the villages and perform in community centers. Usually held in an open-air arena, it combines oratory, group opera, and dance.

The performance, which occupies most of the day, is a competition between two well-rehearsed groups of men and women on a central stage. They wear 19th century French court dress: the men in military coats and the women in evening dress with silk lambas (scarves) around their shoulders.

First comes the kabary, speeches made by a skilled speaker to excuse his inadequacy, praise God, and welcome the rowdy audience. Then the hira gasy offers a morality play that is sung and gestured, advising people to behave well in life so that they can go on to become good ancestors. Finally, the synchronized dancers perform to the music of trumpets, drums, and violins. The winners are judged by audience response and the applause generated.

strings attached lengthways around a hollow bamboo tube. If the strings are attached to a rectangular sound box, it is called a *marovany* ("MAH-ro-VARN"). The instrument looks like a bassoon but is played like a harp to produce rippling chords. An expert player of the valiba is Tombo Daniel from Toamasina.

Many traditional instruments, made of bamboo or a gourd, produce only one note, such as the *kiloloka* ("KEE-lo-LOOK") that whistles shrilly or the traditional Malagasy flute, the *sodina* ("so-DEEN"). Music is often made by a group of players producing harmonies and rhythmic variations as each one creates his single note. The most famous player of the sodina flute is Rakotofra, and his picture is on the 1,000 FMG banknote.

African influence is evident in the many drums, rattles, and sounding animal horns. There are guitars and fiddles too. The more modern popularity of the accordion reflects the recent French colonial era.

The most well-known Malagasy musician is probably Paul Rahasimanana, known as Rossy, who earned his

fame by performing *vaky soava* ("vahk SOOV"), choral music with a strong beat accompanied by hand-clapping. He added instrumental accompaniment and soon became popular, playing in concerts and on the radio. In the 1980s his band toured overseas. His most famous recording was *Island of Ghosts*, which seems a fitting theme for a place so bound up in its respect for the dead. In this piece of music, Rossy combined traditional styles with modern lyrics on the themes of poverty, hope, and love.

In the towns, posters attract local residents to jazz concerts, or to a spectacular fashion show that attracts both men and women. The most successful local groups playing pop music in Malagasy style have been Mahaleo and Tarika Sammy (which made it to the international music world). There are occasional classical music concerts as well.

A man performs a traditional dance in Antananarivo. The country's contact with many cultures has given it a rich legacy of artistic styles and forms of expression.

ARCHITECTURE

Building styles depend on the materials available. Brick and corrugated iron are used on the high plateau where there are hardly any trees left for timber. Coastal homes may have a framework of wooden poles, with walls and roof made of palm fronds, thatch, woven matting, or mud and wattle. Where there is suitable wood, the Malagasy enjoy carving patterned posts or face-boards for verandas and porches.

The compass points of a house are important and each direction has a significance. For example, the north represents power, the south suggests bad influences, and the east is sacred. In the southern part of the house may be the hearth, in a square pit, with cooking pots, ax, and

Wood carving, Madagascar's primary art form, finds expression in wooden houses as well.

firewood set against the south wall. Guests will be seated in the north or northwest of the house, while the northeast corner is sacred to the ancestors, holding objects of ceremonial use. The husband's bed is usually beside the east wall, where he sleeps with his head to the north.

In the cities, houses are built mostly of red brick, but some blocks of plastered concrete and cement are painted cream, green, or an off-white. Antananarivo has some gracious buildings dating from French colonial days; these have tall windows, wrought-iron balconies, and shutters. Middle-income homes have two or three stories, often with the kitchen at the top, living quarters in the middle, and storage space below. Most town houses have wide balconies supported by brick columns and crowned with steep, tiled roofs.

CRAFT

There is an obvious distinction between articles made of natural materials with a long tradition of design behind them, and articles made of recycled modern scrap. Discarded tomato purée tins are made into oil lamps and soft drink cans become brightly colored model cars. Watering cans are made from milk-powder tins and wire is used to create egg baskets or environment-friendly mousetraps that catch the mouse alive, to be eaten or set free elsewhere. French-style, long-handled spades are made from bits of old motor cars. Tires are turned into sandals.

SACRED ART

Madagascar's oldest "art" has a sacred quality. Tomb decorations in wood or stone form the most lasting examples. Mahafaly tombs (in the southwest) are among the most elaborately painted or carved of any on the island. These may include scenes or details from the life of the deceased, or more stylized geometric designs.

The people carve *aloalo* ("a-LOOL"), memorial posts sometimes 6–12 feet high (2–4 m), that are set up on the rectangular tomb or in the grave area. The word aloalo means "shadow of death" and it was originally intended as a resting place for the deceased's soul, so the aloalo and grave area constitute a shrine.

In more recent years, greater realism and even an element of humor has become evident in tomb decorations. The funerary art of the Sakalava (in the west) can be complex, with carved zebu cattle and fanciful birds, sometimes incorporating male and female figures that appear strangely sexual to a Western eye, but that probably represent the notion of rebirth.

Raffia is turned into market baskets with leather handles or hats with wide brims. Rugs are made from raffia and rags. The true craftsmen carve in wood and horn. Woodcarving from Ambositra is famous, as is Betsileo furniture made of valuable hardwoods. The objects created are often practical and include headrests, stools, and walking sticks. Tourists buy boxes with inlaid decoration, model sailboats, and solitaire sets made from semiprecious stones.

In the town of Antaimoro, a decorative papyrus-like paper, with dried flowers embedded in it, is used to make wall-hangings and lampshades. It was originally produced from the pulped bark of the avoha tree, but sisal is used as well.

Women enjoy wearing lambas made from locally produced silk colored with herbal dyes. The silk is woven from silkworms reared on mulberry trees. Particularly attractive is the *lambahoany* ("LAM-ba-OON"), the colorful cloth of the widespread Sakalava tribe. There is also ornamental cloth made of finely woven raffia, and decorative tablecloths and mats are crocheted or embroidered.

Market vendors do not have a set price for their goods, so all transactions involve a fair bit of bargaining. Much of the craftwork on sale is intended for tourists, but the Malagasy like to decorate their houses as well. A serious attempt is being made to stop the sale of items originating from endangered creatures, such as tortoiseshell, crocodile skin, and stuffed lemurs.

Above and opposite: **Colorful straw hats and pottery being sold at the market.**

TEXTILES

Weaving is popular in Madagascar and has distinct features not found anywhere else within the African context. Silk, cotton, wool, raffia, and bast fibers are used alone or in different combinations on the many types of looms found on the island. Malagasy weaving technology appears to carry the mixture of Malayo-Polynesian, African, and Arab influence that is also evident in the people's culture. In Madagascar, weaving is done only by women.

The Merina loom, similar in style to those found in Southeast Asia, does not rely on a fixed structure of weight to create the required tension; instead, it uses the weight of the weaver's body.

Cotton lambas worn by men and women on a wash line.

Most cloth is woven in stripes of different widths and colors. It can have a border decorated with small silver beads. Silk weaving comes mostly from the Merina and Betsileo people; cotton, once widespread, now mainly from the Betsileo; wool is associated with the south; bast with the Merina, Tanala, and Betsileo; and raffia, the fiber most widely used, with the Betsimisaraka, Sakalava, Merina, and Tanala.

The lamba is a large, warp-striped cloth (woven of bast and raffia) that used to be traditional wear throughout the island. It was worn by everyone and removed only when some vigorous task had to be undertaken. Distinct from this common wrap is the lamba mena, the shroud reserved for wrapping dead bodies. The earliest reports indicate that these were always of silk and dyed red. Now the color red is not always predominant, and a shroud may contain colors prescribed by the ombiasy, who determines the most favorable colors for a particular ancestor.

IMPACT OF THE MODERN WORLD

Twentieth century creative expression, such as film directing and photography, have arrived in Madagascar but are still very much in their infancy. However, the printing industry is well established; newspapers are popular and often critical of government policy.

Very little reading material is available for children apart from their school books. An effort has been made, with the help of sponsorship from abroad, to produce a set of eight *Miniboky* booklets: small, square, colorful books for children in the Malagasy language. They depict modern scenes instead of traditional folk tales. In Antananarivo, there is a children's newspaper, *Matsilo* ("mat-SEE-lo"), written mostly in French with a little Malagasy, that is published monthly. The newspaper is filled with snippets of factual information, but has some word puzzles as well.

The *Miniboky* books and *Matsilo* newspaper are targeted at children.

LEISURE

IN MANY COUNTRIES, children always seem to be kicking a soccer ball around or playing a makeshift game of baseball or cricket. But in Madagascar, ball games are absent in most of the rural districts. Soccer, however, is played as a sport in school, as well as volleyball and tennis. So on the high plateau, where more children attend school, more children play organized sports.

ENTHUSIASM FOR SPORTS

Athletics has become increasingly popular over the past 10 years and there are now interprovincial school meets. Students compete at soccer too, using a local stadium in the mornings, with smartly dressed teams and

Left: **Informal cockfight in an eastern village.**

Opposite: **Teenagers playing foosball, popular throughout the country.**

uniformed referee and linesmen. In the evenings and on the weekends, their fathers take over the stadiums for their games. The newspapers keep readers up to date with news of Maradona and other world soccer stars. During the World Cup soccer tournament in 1994, many cafés displayed tablecloths featuring the top teams. Girls as well as boys play the game.

There is increasing enthusiasm for tennis, although it is an expensive sport to organize. Madagascar takes part in the Africa Cup. Cycling is popular, and tourists have discovered that the rough tracks and country roads are ideal for mountain-biking. They also enjoy organized canoe trips on the rivers Tsiribihina and Manambaho in the west. Tennis courts, swimming pools, and golf clubs in Antananarivo and some other major centers are legacies of French colonial occupation. A newly introduced sport is horseracing, with support and interest from South Africa. Newspapers in Antananarivo carry details of handball league championships and table tennis competitions.

Madagascar first participated in the Olympic Games in 1964 and has sent sportsmen to five subsequent Olympics, but has yet to win any medals. However, Dally Randriamptefy, 18, won Madagascar's first gold medal for tennis in the All-Africa Games in Harare in 1995.

LOCAL SPORTS

If in the more traditional areas of Madagascar people seem to show little interest in organized Western-style sports, it does not mean they do not like to show off their athletic prowess and bravery. There are several indigenous sports events. In the northwest cattle country around Morafenobe, there is a form of bullfighting known as *tolon'omby* ("to-lon-OMB"), which resembles an American rodeo. Young men dash among the bulls inside a stockade trying to catch one by the horns (or hump or tail) and hold on as long as possible. The crowd roars its approval at displays of bravery and skill, or jeers if the youngster falls too quickly.

The Sakalava have a style of fighting called *moraingy* ("mor-AIN-gi") where two opponents swing blows at each other with arms and bare fists until one steps back. The fighting is fast and tough, with emphasis on agility. The object is to knock one's opponent flat on his back.

As might be expected from a population closely linked to Indonesia and the East, oriental martial arts are popular, although there are uneasy memories of the 1985 street violence in Antananarivo attributed to kung fu clubs.

Opposite: **Fishers make daily excursions on the crystal clear lakes and sea.**

YOUTH ORGANIZATIONS

There are three Scout organizations—the Scouts of Madagascar, the Unionist Scouts of Madagascar, and the Catholic Boy Scout Association of Madagascar—with a total membership of about 6,500. All three direct their main efforts toward community development, taking an active part in rural education and helping with instruction in adult literacy classes. The Scouts have also helped during national disasters, undertaking relief projects, rescuing farmers during floods, and rounding up cattle to move them to higher ground. Some churches have youth clubs, and the church often acts as the social center for the community.

Fanorona, the traditional game of Madagascar played on a board divided into 32 squares crossed by many diagonal lines.

LIVING IT UP

The board game *fanorona* ("fan-or-OON"), a complicated Malagasy version of checkers, is a national pastime. A complex grid of crisscrossed lines is marked out on the ground (or specially made stone blocks in public arcades) and two opponents move counters, encouraged by a crowd. Each player tries to "eat" his opponent's pieces. It is a leisurely game that does not require speed, for there are traps everywhere. The philosophy of fanorona rests on the idea that life presents many possibilities. The result most prized by experienced players is a draw, for the goal is not direct aggression, but to stop one's opponent from moving. There is even a national fanorona organization.

Another game is katra, which involves shifting piles of stones around the board until the player has won all the stones.

The café version of football, *foosball* ("FOOS-ball"), with rows of wooden players on little metal rods, is highly popular with younger men.

They play pool or table tennis as well. The departure lounge of a small-town airport is sometimes used as a social club in the evenings. Men gather there for a beer or to play cards or dominoes.

Young children play hopscotch, scratching an eight-square pattern in the dust and hopping on one foot, while kicking a piece of wood on to the next square. Older ones listen to imported music on cassettes or twist happily at the local discotheque. Antananarivo has about a dozen discotheques and most towns have at least one.

POPULAR MEDIA

Young people enjoying a basketball game.

The government-controlled Radio-Television Malagasy broadcasts radio programs in Malagasy and French, and four to six hours of television a day. On most days television viewing starts at noon and includes Bugs Bunny and Tom and Jerry cartoons, sports programs, news in French and Malagasy, and films from France and the United States. Not many homes have television, so an evening's entertainment may be to go to a "video café" to watch television or a video film.

There are few cinemas apart from those in Antananarivo and the larger towns. In the capital city, the Albert Camus Cultural Center has theater programs and concerts, varying from classical to jazz and rock. Films are shown at the Alliance Française center (found in many towns) and several embassies in Antananarivo.

FESTIVALS

ALTHOUGH THERE ARE RELIGIOUS AND POLITICAL festivals imposed by colonial influence and contact with the Western world, there is a movement to establish more festivals connected with the natural cycles of the year. In some places, for example, a Festival of Trees or Festival of Rice is held in February to mark the harvest.

This appeals to people in the rural areas where the preparation, growth, and harvesting of rice mark the progress of time far more memorably than any public holidays. A successful rice harvest ensures survival, so it is hardly surprising that common expressions concerning time refer to how long it takes to cook a pot of rice, or the time it takes for rice seedlings to sprout.

Other holidays mark religious or political events. If a holiday falls on a Thursday, it is extended to Friday to create a longer weekend.

Religious festivals are observed by the Catholic and Protestant churches with worship services in much the same way as anywhere else in the world. The Malagasy have adopted from the French Catholics their love of incense, processions, and ceremonial rituals. They observe Christmas and Easter, the main Christian festivals, in conventional style. Father Christmas is known as *le Bonhomme Noël* in French or *Dadabenoely* ("DAH-da-bay-NOWEL") in Malagasy, and is portrayed in the usual red outfit trimmed with white fur despite the heat of a tropical summer in December.

Opposite: **Festival exuberance in colorful clothes and painted faces.**

Below: **Winnowing rice. The government encourages the blending of old and new cultural expressions. The celebration of the rice harvest in the Festival of Rice is one of the seasonal festivals introduced recently.**

Ry tanindrazanay malala ô! ("RAY TAN-in-dra-ZAH-nay ma-LAHL ob") — "Oh, Our Beloved Fatherland" is the national anthem of Madagascar.

POLITICALLY MOTIVATED HOLIDAYS

On March 29 people remember the 1947 rebellion led by Joseph Raseta and Joseph Ravoahangy against French domination. The insurrection was crushed and thousands of Malagasy were killed: some estimates say as many as 80,000. However, it was the beginning of a popular movement that eventually led to the country's longed-for independence in 1960.

This is celebrated as Independence Day on June 26. There is a week-long program of events leading to June 26, when schoolchildren parade with banners proclaiming the republic's motto, "Fatherland, Liberty, Equity." They sing the national anthem and watch the national flag being raised. Speeches, singing, and processions follow, and there is usually

OFFICIAL PUBLIC HOLIDAYS

January 1	New Year's Day
March 29	Insurrection Day
April*	Good Friday, Easter Sunday and Monday
May 1	Labor Day
May 25	Organization of African Unity Day
May*	Ascension Day
May*	Pentecost Monday
June 26	Independence Day
August 15	Assumption
November 1	All Saints' Day
December 25	Christmas Day
December 30	Republic Day, or Anniversary of the Democratic Republic of Madagascar

* The exact date varies from year to year

a Grand Ball and family feasting in the evening. The Anniversary of the Democratic Republic of Madagascar is celebrated in similar style on December 30.

The internationally observed Labor Day on May 1 was instituted when communist ideals were being copied during the presidency of Didier Ratsiraka, but it is now observed as Workers' Day by the present trade unions.

Madagascar is a member of the Organization of African Unity (OAU) and a member of the United Nations, so May 25, which is the Organization of African Unity Day, is an opportunity to emphasize the country's political links with the African mainland. The Malagasy do not consider themselves to be Africans, but because of the legacy of French colonial rule, the island has developed political, economic, and cultural links with the French-speaking countries of Western Africa. It is also regarded as advantageous to have trade links with the mainland.

Processions, parades, and feasting accompany the festivities and special events observed by the people.

TRADITIONAL FESTIVITIES

The New Year is Madagascar's most popular festival and a time for gift-giving. Recently, there has been a desire to bring back traditional customs including *Alahamady* ("a-lah-MARD"), or the first new moon in the first month of the Malagasy New Year.

Two generations of royal descendants at a New Year festival in Ambohi-manga.

In Antananarivo it is celebrated as a two-day festival. People in bright holiday clothes throng to the highest point in the city, the sacred royal hill of Ambohimanga, and gather in the royal enclosure around what was once the Queen's Palace, with rowdy music playing. It is fady to bring alcohol to such a ceremony or wear shoes because they impart a sense of superiority. An invocation is made to the ancestors, using an age-old formula. Some go into a trance and relay messages and prayers to individual ancestors.

After a night of rejoicing, New Year's Day starts with a Christian hymn. Such a mix of traditional belief and Christianity is not unusual. Two zebu

THE MALAGASY CALENDAR

In traditional Malagasy culture, time and place come together in the home. Even without conventional education, country folk can count the passing of the lunar months by noting the four walls and corners of their house in relation to their compass points. That, supposedly, is why there are no round huts in Madagascar as there are in Africa. The year starts with *Alahamady* (New Year) in the northeast. The different months hold differing predictions of vintana (fortune) according to the phase of the moon.

cattle are sacrificed by attendants wearing something red, as it is the royal color and a symbol of power. Those fortunate enough to be anointed with the cattle's blood feel assured that their prayers will be answered.

The famadihana (reburial) ceremony should be undertaken every year for one or more ancestors, but few families can afford this. By law, this ritual must take place between June and October, presumably because they are the cooler months and the opening of a tomb will present less of a health hazard in terms of unpleasant odors and disease.

Circumcision is practiced in Madagascar as a fertility rite. It is performed on boys as young as 5 or 6 years old, mostly during June to September, and is not regarded as the gateway between adolescence and adulthood as in many parts of the African mainland. Among the Antaimoro people in the southeast, the ceremony is observed once every seven years and the feast may go on for several days. There are specific fady rules: uncircumcised boys are not "men" and may not marry, nor be laid in the family tomb. While still boys, they must not handle sharp iron instruments, which seems a sensible precaution for young children.

Happy children in a west coast primary school. Circumcision is commonly performed on boys before they reach the age of 10.

FOOD

FRENCH CUISINE SEEMS THE ONE COLONIAL LEGACY for which the Malagasy should be grateful. They cook beef, chicken, and seafood exquisitely for their European residents or foreign visitors. For themselves, they insist on having rice three times a day. Tradition requires that the oldest member of the family drinks first, but should always stop eating before the young, so as to leave enough for them.

RICE

The Malagasy eat about a pound (half a kilogram) of rice, which they call *vary* ("VAR"), daily and consider themselves poorly treated if it is not available. For variety, they cook it differently each time: more watery at breakfast, and drier for lunch and supper, when it is served with onion or another vegetable. A Malagasy cook does not decide whether or not to have rice, but merely chooses what to have with it. Everything goes with rice—perhaps a boiled egg, or a few bits of stewed or boiled zebu beef, fish, or chicken. With this may come a small bowl of *rano vola* ("RAHN-o VOOL," which is water boiled with the residue in the rice pot) or *brêdes* ("BREED," or boiled greens) to finish off the plate of rice.

Rice is considered the only substantial food, but it is also a feature of Malagasy living. Growing rice requires more people than one household can provide, so families have to be friends with each other. They join together to trample the ground to prepare it for the planting of seeds, take turns in "rice watching"

Opposite: **Exotic dishes make the most of the ingredients provided by the island's bountiful waters.**

Below: **Vendor selling palm marrow.**

A feast of local favorites.

(making sure that the birds do not eat the sown seed and that cattle or wild pigs do not trample the young plants), and harvest the crop. Even pounding the rice with a heavy wooden pestle can be turned into a sort of dancing game in which a circle of four to six women throw the pestle across to one another while keeping up a steady rhythm.

STEWS AND SAUCES

Apart from rice, the national meat dish (for those who can afford meat) is *romazava* ("room-a-ZAHV"), a beef and vegetable stew in thin gravy with a hint of ginger, served with rice, spinach-like greens, and perhaps a salad. Another favorite is *ravitoto* ("RAH-vee-TOOT-o"), which is manioc leaves with fried pork. Meat is a luxury, so small mammals often end up in the cooking pot. One local official remarked sadly, "Soon, all the lemurs will be extinct because they are so tasty." Villagers usually taste beef very occasionally, perhaps only after a ceremonial slaughter of one of their precious zebu.

Although their cooking is seldom strongly spiced, the Malagasy enjoy mouth-searing sauces such as a hot, pickled vegetable curry, a fiery pepper sauce, or *rougaille* ("roo-GUY"), made from tomatoes, ginger, onions, lemon, and hot peppers.

They bake their bread, *mofo* ("MOOF"), in long thin loaves like French baguettes. In many villages cassava or manioc root (which looks like a yam but tastes different) is used as a bread substitute.

The influence of their ancestral lands is found in the popularity of Chinese and Indian restaurants. They have adapted the noodle-rich Chinese soup into a most filling meal with greens and bits of seafood or chicken, often served with a helping of soy sauce.

Chicken is on the menu in many flavors and so is turkey, a bird not restricted by any local *fady*. However, only gray-haired people may keep geese since they have gray hair that counters the *fady* of the gray geese. Coastal fishers add crab, crayfish, shrimp, prawns, oysters, and many varieties of fish to their menu, although most of the catch is sold to hotels and restaurants rather than eaten at home.

EATING OUT

Going to a restaurant is an indulgence for the rich. A lunchtime excursion is not as popular as an evening one because of the midday heat. In the evening, after a drink perhaps on an open veranda, dinner may last from 7 p.m. until late at night. The menu might include *paella* ("pi-ELL-a"), a mound of seasoned rice surrounded by prawns, pieces of chicken, hunks of crab, and lobster claws with a tomato, onion, and shrimp sauce.

Drying stacks of fish around a fire.

Those who prefer a less expensive meal will find fastfood outlets on street corners, where rows of street vendors offer snacks in abundance. There are also curious relics of French occupation in the form of tea rooms selling sandwiches, sausage rolls, cakes, and pastries.

Fruits and vegetables tempt shoppers at a market.

SATISFYING A SWEET TOOTH

Dessert is easily found in Madagascar: from October to December, there are fresh pineapples, lychees, strawberries, mangoes, and bananas growing wild that can be picked and eaten. In the markets, oranges, peaches, pears, apricots, and apples are available. Coconut is eaten in fresh slices, drunk (as water from the nut), or cooked with brown toffee into sweets. The Malagasy serve bananas in many ways: fried in batter, cooked inside a pancake, or flamed in rum, which can be considered the national dessert. Nibblers buy slices of *parique* ("pa-REEK"), made from peanuts, rice, and sugar, and wrapped and baked in banana leaves. There is a local dark chocolate with a bitter flavor, and peanut brittle or loose peanuts are always available.

Malagasy cheeses are made almost exclusively in the south central highlands, and there is a delicious pepper cheese. Zebu cattle provide little milk, so there are few other dairy products.

MASHED BANANA FRITTERS

3 large, ripe bananas
4 ounces (112 g) granulated sugar
4 tablespoons milk
2 tablespoons cornstarch, perhaps more
1 teaspoon ground nutmeg
vegetable oil for frying

Peel and cut the bananas and mash them in a bowl. Add the rest of the ingredients (except the oil) and mix together thoroughly. The mixture should be thick and not too mushy. Heat the oil in a frying pan. If your first spoonful of banana mixture burns, turn the heat down. Cook the mixture in small dollops, turning to brown on both sides. Drain on absorbent paper before serving.

Exotic cocktails and fruity wines add to the island's tourist appeal.

DRINKS

Although the poor have no choice, the water that comes out of the communal taps is seldom safe to drink by Western standards. The common beverage is rice water boiled in the empty rice pot, flavored by grains of burnt rice (boiling makes it safer to drink than water from the tap or river). Fresh milk is not easily available so the Malagasy drink their coffee or tea without milk, providing a portion of sticky condensed milk for the strange foreigners who seem to require it.

Coconut milk is a popular drink in the coastal towns; mix it with rum and one has *punch aux cocos*. There are several varieties of commercially distilled rum, often with added vanilla, honey, or lemon grass flavors. Variations of crude alcohol made from rice, sugarcane, coconut, or lychees are meant for local consumption. The national beer is a lager named Three Horses, and there is a stronger brew called Gold.

Fruity wines from local vineyards such as Domremy, d'Antsirabe, Betsileo, and Côte de Fianer come as red, white, rosé, and gris (a dry-tasting, pinkish wine).

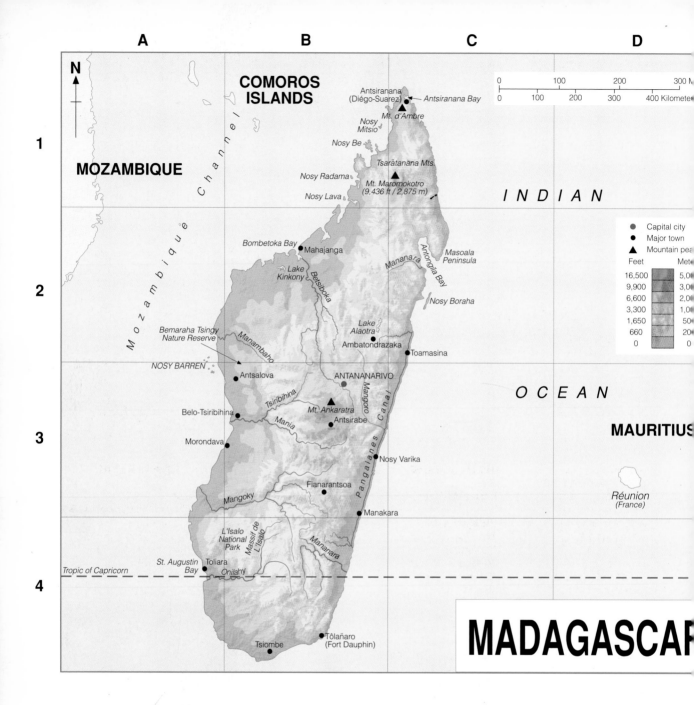

A   **B**   **C**   **D**

N

**COMOROS
ISLANDS**

Antsiranana
(Diégo-Suarez) ← *Antsiranana Bay*
▲ *Mt. d'Ambre*

*Nosy
Mitsio*

1

MOZAMBIQUE

Nosy Be

Mozambique Channel

Tsarätanana Mts.

Nosy Radama
▲ Mt. Maromokotro
(9,436 ft / 2,875 m)

Nosy Lava

INDIAN

Bombetoka Bay
● Mahajanga

Mananara

Antongila Bay

*Masoala
Peninsula*

*Lake
Kinkony*

Betsiboka

2

Nosy Boraha

*Bemaraha Tsingy
Nature Reserve*

Manambaho

*Lake
Alaotra*
● Ambatondrazaka
● Toamasina

NOSY BARREN

● Antsalova

ANTANANARIVO

Mangoro

OCEAN

Tsiribihina

▲ Mt. Ankaratra
● Antsirabe

Pangalanes Canal

MAURITIUS

● Belo-Tsiribihina

Mania

3

● Morondava

Nosy Varika

Mangoky

● Fianarantsoa

*Réunion
(France)*

● Manakara

*L'Isalo
National
Park*

*Massif de
L'Isalo*

Mananara

Tropic of Capricorn

*St. Augustin
Bay*
Toliara

Onilahy

4

● Tsiombe

● Tôlañaro
(Fort Dauphin)

MADAGASCAR

●	Capital city
●	Major town
▲	Mountain peak

Feet		Meters
16,500		5,000
9,900		3,000
6,600		2,000
3,300		1,000
1,650		500
660		200
0		0

0   100   200   300 M
0   100   200   300   400 Kilometers

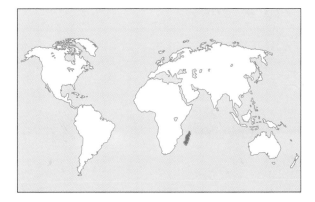

QUICK NOTES

OFFICIAL NAME
Democratic Republic of Madagascar
(*Repoblika Demokratika n'i Madagaskar*)

LAND AREA
226,598 square miles (586,889 square km),
including offshore islands

POPULATION
13.5 million

LAND REGIONS
Antananarivo (capital) and six provinces:
Antsiranana, Fianarantsoa, Mahajanga,
Toamasina, Toliara, and Tôlañaro

CAPITAL
Antananarivo

IMPORTANT CITIES
Toamasina, Mahajanga, and Fianarantsoa

HIGHEST POINT
Mt. Maromokotro (9,436 feet/2,875 meters)

MAJOR RIVERS
Betsiboka, Tsiribihina, Mangoky, and Onilahy

MAJOR LAKE
Alaotra

OFFICIAL LANGUAGES
Malagasy and French

NATIONAL FLAG
A vertical white strip next to the flagmast taking
up one-third of the flag; the other two thirds
divided horizontally into red (upper) and green
(lower)

NATIONAL SYMBOL
The traveler's palm

MAJOR RELIGION
Christianity, with a form of ancestor worship in
many areas

CURRENCY
Malagasy franc (FMG) divided into 100 centimes
(US$1 = 3,950 FMG)

MAIN EXPORTS
Coffee, cloves, vanilla, sugar, textiles, and
petroleum products.

IMPORTANT HOLIDAYS
New Year's Day, Easter, Workers' Day (May 1),
Independence Day (June 26), Christmas, and
Anniversary of the Democratic Republic of
Madagascar (December 30).

IMPORTANT POLITICAL LEADERS
Philibert Tsiranana (president of the First
   Republic)
Didier Ratsiraka (president of the Second
   Republic and current president)
Albert Zafy (president of the Third Republic,
   recently removed from office)

GLOSSARY

Alabamady ("a-lah-MARD")
First new moon in first month of the Malagasy New Year.

aloalo ("a-LOOL")
Carved memorial posts.

côtiers ("COH-ti-ay")
Coastal people.

Dadabenoely ("DAH-da-bay-NOWEL")
Father Christmas.

fady ("FAH-di")
Forbidden.

fanorona ("fan-or-OON")
Malagasy board game.

faritany ("FAR-i-TARN")
Provinces.

fokonolona ("FOOK-on-o-LOON")
Village social committees.

fokontany ("FOOK-on-TARN")
Localized community rule.

foosball ("FOOS-ball")
"Table" football.

haiteny ("HAY-ten-i")
Traditional style of love poetry.

khat ("KAT")
Plant whose leaves are chewed as a stimulant.

lamba ("LAM-ba")
All-purpose garment.

mofo ("MOOF")
Malagasy bread.

ombiasy ("om-bi-ASH")
Traditional healer.

paella ("pi-ELL-a")
Seasoned rice with prawns and chicken.

parique ("pa-REEK")
Snack made from peanuts, rice, and sugar.

pousse-pousse ("POOSS-POOSS")
Cart for passengers or goods, pulled by a man.

rano vola ("RAHN-o VOOL")
Water boiled with the residue in the rice pot.

rougaille ("roo-GUY")
Sauce made from tomatoes, ginger, onions, lemon, and hot peppers.

sodina ("so-DEEN")
Traditional Malagasy flute.

taxi-brousse ("TAK-si-BROOSS")
Minibus or pick-up truck.

toaka gasy ("TOH-ka GASH")
Illegal homemade rum.

tsingy ("TSING-i")
Sharp limestone pinnacles.

valiba ("va-LEE-b")
Musical instrument resembling a zither.

vintana ("vin-TARN")
Person's fortune.

BIBLIOGRAPHY

Hilary Bradt. *Guide to Madagascar*. United States/United Kingdom. Bradt Publications/Globe Pequot Press, 1994.

Madagascar—In Pictures. Minneapolis. Lerner Publications, 1988.

Morris, Neil. *The World's Top Ten Islands*. London. Belitha Press, 1995.

Swaney, Deanna and Robert Willcox. *Madagascar & Comoros*. Australia. Lonely Planet, 1994.

INDEX

INDEX

INDEX

PHOTO CREDITS